Dear Alicia,

This whole book is *"I-this"* and *"I-that."*

Everything that happened, though: It was *we*. Always has been, always is, and always will be.

You were, all through it, a stunning exhibition of love, strength, vision, and courage.

Thank you, honey.

Love,

Keith

unmediated
un · me · di · at · ed

---

*without anyone or anything intervening
or acting as an intermediary.*

Un Mediated

Simple **Faith**. Pure **Love**.

Endorsements

I sat down thinking I would start reading your manuscript today and then pick it up again tomorrow morning. But I just kept on reading. Because I could not put it down. Your voice takes on the form of a lot of rapid-fire, short, but very compelling and deep thoughts, all of which connect and flow together beautifully.

Dr. Christy Berghoef

* * *

I absolutely loved it. I started crying on page 40 I sobbed on page 65, and then laughed and cried till the end.

Stacey Graham

* * *

Keith Mannes was a beloved Evangelical pastor . . . until he spoke to a reporter and told the truth. That act of courageous truth-telling changed his career and his life. If you dare to listen to his passionate and well-told story, it might change your life as well. Especially this year!

Brian D. McLaren
author of Life After Doom

Keith Mannes has a unique and compelling voice. It's real, authentic, honest, and captivating. And the story he tells is compelling, heart-breaking, painful and, sadly, widely shared.

Mannes takes a hard look at his faith and finds God not in church but in the faces and stories of the people he works with. In the end, he discovers a richer, more robust faith, letting go of "church-ianity" and embracing something more authentic, closer to what Jesus taught (and embodied).

Doug Brouwer
author of *How to Become a Multicultural Church & Chasing After Wind: A Pastor's Life.*

Table of Contents

Forword 1
Why I Wrote This 3
Quick, Important Things 5

    The Impossible Situation 5
    Hospice and HIPPAA 6
    Codes and Clicks 6
    My Terms 6

Section One
Fire In My Bones
Rejecting Religious Trumpism and Leaving Ministry

    Clown Trailing Smoke 14
    The Day I Didn't Roll 14
    The Game Jesus Never Played 15
    By Spiritual Heritage, I Had to Speak 16
    Jesus, Not Big Enough 22
    The Elders, Suffering Me 22
    The Text That Signaled the End 23
    In The Rain at Kitty Hawk 25
    The Church's Liars and Cheaters 26
    My Unpardonable Sin 28
    Five Minutes of Fame 30

Section Two
Ninety-Foot Statue
Exactly Why I Oppose Religious Trumpism

    The Core of It 34
    The Answer When the Elder Asked, "Why?" 35
    Answer to the Denominational Official 36
    What the African Refugee Said 36
    Examples of The Church's Trump Worship 37

UnMediated

A Church in Dementia 39
Lament 41
Summary of Section Two 42

Section Three
Stones In The Windshield
Prior Events Whch Began to Weaken my Faith in The Church

The Man Who Couldn't Speak 46
When Alicia Confronted the School Board 48
We, the Stone-Shattered 52
You are Not Alone 53

Section Four
Rebuilding Life at Sixty
Career and Religion Change

You Will Suffer Loss 58

Section Five
Soul in a Snowy Ditch
What it felt like to be spiritually lost

An Awful Conclusion about My Life 62
I Became a Person Without Faith 63
The Confounding Mystery of Jason's Faith 65
Feeling Like a Nuthin' 67
Leave the Place Where Jesus is Not 68
God Will Send You People 69
What I Don't Do about Lostness 71

Section Six
Friends in Forsaken Places
Where, Sometimes, I Encounter Jesus

God Tugs at Me Through People 76
God in Nearly-Dead People 76
My Church Math No Longer Adds Up 77
The Cosmic Good Samaritan 81
Theology Later 82
The Divine Synapse............................. 84
Jayne's Kiss 85
Jesus in Weakness 86

Simple **Faith**. Pure **Love**.

    Sacrament from a Tin Can 87
    Locked Dementia Unit 88
    It Cannot Be Wrong to Seek a New Way 91
    Why I Keep Saying "Sometimes" 91

Section Seven
Dumpster Theology
Thoughts on God and Faith

    Jesus Alone . . . 97
    Jesus First (Not Moses, Paul, or Preachers) 98
    Abandon the Abraham Project 100
    Unity, Wayne's Way 101
    Bobblehead Jesus 103
    I Reject Christian-Based Violence & Aggression . . . 104
    I Reject the Gospel of the Four Guys 106
    What Is "The Gospel?" 108
    Unconditional Love 109
    Simple Joy 111
    Hell and Heaven, Here and Now 113
    Still a Mess 114

Section Eight
What if I'm Wrong?

    The Tragedy We Already Know 118
    Writing a New Story 121

Section Nine
Safety & Spritual Freedon for a Lost Person

    Explaining How I Landed in a Church 126

Conclusion

    Summary 133
    Suffering to stand against Religious Trumpism 134

Endnotes 137

Acknowledgements 141

About the Author 143

UnMediated

Simple **Faith**. Pure **Love**.

Copyright © 2024
Keith A. Mannes / Synapse
All Rights Reserved

All rights reserved. No part of this publication may be reproduced, stored in an automated database, or made public in any form or by any means, electronically, mechanically, by photocopying, recording, or in any other way, without the prior written permission of the copyright holder.

ISBN: 979-8-9899066-7-3 - *hardcover*
ISBN: 979-8-9899066-6-6 - *softcover*
ISBN: 979-8-9899066-8-0 - *e-book*

---

keithamannes.com

Edited by
Jacob Schepers & Rod Colburn

Photography
Christine Berghoef

Book Design & Production
timmyroland.com

Spiritual Growth Without the Interference of Christianity

UnMediated

Simple **Faith**. Pure **Love**.

Keith A. Mannes

Synapse

UnMediated

Simple **Faith**. Pure **Love**.

Forword

Keith Mannes is a truth-teller.

He communicates in love, and with urgency.

Keith's story is at once personal and intense, and it is also universal dealing with the question, "how does a leader change their conviction and priorities?"

Many of us have been told that "holding the line;" "never giving in;" "being strong and steadfast" is the sign of true conviction.

Keith shows us the kind of path we may need to walk when the Spirit of God begins to move.

This is a story reminiscent of the great transformations of the Biblical text and the history of faith.

This book is a field-guide for those who know they must stay open and change in order the stay true to their faith.

Doug Pagitt
Vote Common Good

UnMediated

Simple **Faith**. Pure **Love**.

Simple **Faith**. Pure **Love**.

Why I Wrote This

Thank you for giving this book your time and attention. I wrote it for three reasons, the third of which both frightens and emboldens me:

First, sometimes people ask me why I left ministry with such heat and storm. I tell them. They become still and thoughtful. They express some kind of incredulity. They say, "You should write about that." So I did.

Second, people ask me about their own faith, and about church, because they feel lost and uprooted. When I share with them how and when I experience God, their body language expresses relief. Apparently, people feel some spiritual peace as I share my story and faith concepts. I hope you feel some of that, too. Despite all the hard things I will say about religion, I am not trying to wreck anybody's faith. This book is really for people whose faith is already wrecked, and don't know what to do about it. Maybe my faith story will help yours.

The third reason I wrote this: There is a religion stomping and bludgeoning its way across North America which claims to represent Jesus but is anti-Jesus. It is dangerous, and even deadly. It is not a time to whistle while passing by, to sit comfy in a church pew enjoying smooth sermons and soothing praise teams. It is a time to receive the message of

UnMediated

Jesus (peace, compassion, non-violence) and then lay your life down to represent it in soul and spirit, and with your voice.

This is the story of how my house of sand fell with a great crash. I lost my old faith and am cobbling together a new one. I have stitched together a personal theology and life-practice. It's just a flimsy tent, the loose ends of it flapping in the wind, but within it, sometimes, I find Jesus. Huddling here by this feeble candle against the wailing wind outside, I encounter God and find moments of holiness, without Christianity.

I wish this for you as well. If these words help you find spiritual peace and freedom, I will be thankful.

Gratefully,

Keith A. Mannes

Keith A. Mannes

Simple **Faith**. Pure **Love**.

Quick. Important Things

The Impossible Situation

In October of 2020, I initiated a divorce from the last church I pastored. Most of the congregation was good and abundantly generous to me and to my wife, Alicia. I loved the congregation. I loved the elders of the church especially, who gave their best to support me. What I did hurt them. They suffered because of me. It wasn't their fault. Please think of them, as I do, with heartfelt kindness.

As you will see, we were in an impossible situation. To get us out of it, I activated my denomination's pastor-church separation process. We were like a plane on fire with only one engine left, and no landing gear. I was trying to glide this doomed relationship down, hoping to avoid a total crash.

Later, I also divorced the denomination of my upbringing, within which I had served for over thirty years as an ordained pastor. As I explain, I thank God for the legacy of faith given to me by a beautiful host of Christian people.

I caused all this damage for what I believe is the simple gospel of Jesus, in opposition to the poisonous religion which had hijacked The Church broadly. I did it so that I could publicly oppose Religious Trumpism.

Hospice and HIPPAA

These days, I am a Hospice Chaplain. In the stories

that follow all the names have been changed and the circumstances altered enough to protect the identities of the people I visit. I did this not just for my hospice patients but for all the true stories I tell in this book.

Codes and Clicks

At the bottom of some pages you will find QR codes and other information to help you see for yourself the pictures, videos, and writings to which I refer.

My Terms

Christianity

It seems to me, at this moment in our history, and in this moment in my life, that Christianity is a thought process and a world power system boiling up from underneath layer upon layer of human, mangled interpretations of the Bible and of Jesus. Just too many layers. I avoid the word "Christian" when identifying myself.

The Church

Capital "T" and "C." I am using this word to speak 1: of an earthly, visible institution of Christianity and 2: the 81% of American church goers who supported Donald Trump originally and that percentage which still identifies with the theology of the Religious Right in North America. What I call "The Church," others call the "White Evangelical Church in North America," or "the White Nationalist Church." In our time, "The Church" is a complicated entity. It contains both humble and generous believers, and, lately, wild-eyed religious zealots, hellbent on takeover and domination.

Simple **Faith**. Pure **Love**.

Years ago I saw a church cartoon, about a salesman in a car lot. To the prospective buyers, he was saying something like, "Now, this bus is perfect for churches. It has three steering wheels, eight gas pedals, and twenty sets of brakes." I thought it was cute.

These days, there's nothing funny about it.

The Church bus in North America has been hijacked by religious extremists. They have a death grip on the steering wheels. They see themselves as Old Testament Israelites, and think America is Israel. Therefore, they believe in conquering and subjugating sinners. They use violent language and imagery and seem quite comfortable with the idea of killing people in God's name.

You don't believe me, maybe.

In early 2024, a pastor from my former denomination re-posted an article on his blog. The article was written by Rev. Joseph Rigney.[1] He references Bible stories about Old Testament priests thrusting spears through sexual sinners and cutting down idolaters with swords. The problem today, Rigney says, is feminine empathy. The solution is for men to have no empathy for sin and to be like Old Testament priests. Nowhere in the piece does Rigney mention Jesus.

Pastors like Rigney, and like the pastor re-posting his article, are promoting messages of religious violence

---

1- For the text of the article promoting Old Testament violence, see Joseph Rigney, "Empathy, Feminism, and the Church" in *American Reformer* (January 26, 2024). *https://americanreformer.org/2024/01/empathy-feminism-and-the-church*

and takeover. Religious zealots like them have joined forces and have taken over the steering wheel of The Church. They are hellbent, also, on taking over the United States government and ruling our lives with Old Testament severity.

Their dream has become the living nightmare in my county – the infamous Ottawa County, Michigan you may have heard about.[2] We are afflicted with minority rule. Religious extremists have commandeered our local government and have attacked and dismantled any public services they deem as liberal.

In my former denomination, also, religious pastors like this have seized control and are kicking out any pastor, elder, or deacon who is supportive of LGBTQ+ persons.

To better understand this aspect of The Church, please read:

Jesus and John Wayne, by Kristin DuMez.

Or, watch the film *God and Country,* directed by Dan Partland and produced by Rob Reiner.[3] (Or, at least read a review of the film by Christy Berghoef.[4])

2- For a snapshot of Ottawa Impact in my County, see Sam Landstra, "Deeply Religious, Divided: Ottawa Impact and the Christians in Their County" from Fox17, January 5, 2024. *https://www.fox17online.com/news/local-news/lakeshore/ottawa/deeply-religious-divided-ottawa-impact-and-the-christians-in-their-county*

3- For the film trailer for *God and Country,* see "God and Country – Official Trailer (2024)." YouTube, uploaded by IGN Movie Trailers, 8 December 2023. *https://www.youtube.com/watch?v=-MFQ2uESrjU*

Simple **Faith**. Pure **Love**.

Sure, there are other Christians on the bus who are not dangerous. However, *they are riding along*. They have chosen to believe far-right religious leaders who have told them Donald Trump is a God-fearing man and a fervent believer in Jesus. They are appeasing the religious extremists. This is "The Church" in our day. This book is a confrontation with it. It is your invitation to seek and find peace with God apart from it.

Pastors

I like pastors and honor them. The ones I know and admire view themselves as servants.

The Trump years have been excruciating for good pastors. I feel conflicted and convicted when I see their courage, because I left, and they stayed. My respect has only increased for them, because these committed women and men of God have stood in this horrendous moment and continued to preach and live in a way that resembles Christ.

However, as I will describe, many other pastors have either capitulated to Trumpism or are using the name of God for the sake of their own sense of power.

4- For a review of the Film God and Country, see "God and Country" by Christy Berghoef in Reformed Journal, March 20, 2024.
https://reformedjournal.com/god-and-country

UnMediated

Suspended by
UnMediated Love

My daughter, on her windowsill, has a tiny plant which grows while hanging in midair. In an electromagnetic field of energy, a small bowl gently spins. In the bowl, there is soil, and in the soil, a seedling. The seedling is nourished while floating. It is utterly suspended.

If someone interferes—jabs a finger at the little plant, or gropes with their hand in the circle of energy which upholds it—the field of energy is broken, and the bowl crashes down.

This gently suspended seedling is an image of you, suspended lovingly in the spiritual energy of God. I think this is how Jesus thought of you: Your soul, alive, not born of religious descendancy or human decision or anyone else's intentions.

Simple **Faith**. Pure **Love**.

If, however, a preacher or potentate or some religious force jams a groping hand into that sacred space – deigns to reach in and take something from your soul or to impose human control upon it – that sacred energy is violated.

Here is what I believe: You are of God. From the beginning the flowering of your soul is a divine, direct, and unmediated process.

The purpose of this book is to strengthen your resolve and your confidence to reside in the love of God without human interference, and to reject anything less.

Just picture this: You, even in whatever may be your earthly sufferings, nourished and carried.

Suspended in the loving energy of God.

Simple. Pure.

No preacher. No church.

Just you.

Start there. Remain there. It is enough.

UnMediated

Simple **Faith**. Pure **Love**.

SECTION ONE
Fire In My Bones
Rejecting Religious Trumpism & Leaving Ministry

UnMediated

Clown Trailing Smoke

In a circus, there is a clown who runs around, chased by other clowns, until finally he scampers into a cannon to hide. Someone lights the fuse, the cannon goes "poof," and the clown flies.

I am that pastor-clown, except that I crawled into the cannon of my own volition, reached around, and lit the fuse myself. I haven't landed yet. That's me: Sailing, flailing, and trailing smoke. Yet, as I explain later, spiritually free.

The Day I Didn't Roll

When I was eight years old, some older boys encircled me on our school's baseball diamond. From somewhere, they had buckets of water, which they poured on me. They commanded me to kneel and roll in the dirt, "or else." It was evening; there was no one else around.

I look back on the scene in slow motion. Without a hand laid upon me, with no one shoving me or hitting me, I lowered myself to the ground, flopping from my stomach to my back. The bullies left, cackling. I stood up with the grit of the infield stuck to my wet clothes.

For thirty years of ordained ministry, I kept on lowering myself, rolling in the grit of people's religious expectations. When I was sixty years old, suddenly, surprisingly, for once at least, I didn't.

Simple **Faith**. Pure **Love**.

The Game Jesus Never Played

In a coffee shop, I overheard a church shopper describe how he made his choice. He had carefully surveyed the pastor's sermons. "I've listened to six of them, and I haven't heard anything yet that I disagree with." How tragic.

To grow and maintain a church, pastors must preach to a bandwidth of agreement. You have talk about Jesus in a way that pleases people. Russell Moore, in his book *Losing Our Religion*, tells of a pastor-friend who described for him how to "play the game." The pastor-friend said, "You give them the 90 percent of the red meat they expect, and then you can do the 10 percent of side stuff that you want to do, on immigrants or whatever."[5] That's it: A game of bandwidth, entertainment, and manipulation.

Which is a game Jesus never played. He did not lift his voice to say, after feeding the five thousand, "Y'all show up next week, same time, same place, and I'll toss out free bagels."

He could have gathered large crowds with bread and circuses, like churches do today with Starbucks, donuts, pizza, singers, and light shows. One woman even told me recently about her church, which, she said, "has a nautical theme." In contrast, consider this

---

5- See Russell Moore's *Losing Our Religion* (Sentinel 2023), 7.

title to an article by Amar D. Peterman: "Taylor Swift Needs Fog Machines. God Does Not."[6]

Jesus, rejecting the manipulations of religion, shoo-shoo-ed his disciples away from the crowds after the bread miracle. He made them get into a boat and ushered them into isolation, darkness, life-risk, and suffering. Then, instead of standing around to soak up the crowd's fickle adulation, Jesus went up on a mountain alone. Regularly he turned to the throngs following him and said something offensive to thin the herd. Jesus rolled for no one.

Since 2016, if pastors want to survive ministry, they must play along with Donald Trump's wicked games and roll around in the dirt, groveling for the approval and the tithes of his religious devotees.

In October of 2020, I rejected that life.

By Spiritual Heritage, I Had to Speak

I remember how my people were and thank God for them.

My very existence is a product of The Church. I was conceived after a prayer offered from a church sanctuary. My mother already had a three-year-old daughter. Yet my mom was asking God for a son, too. Like most mothers from among my people, my mom

6- See Amar D. Peterman's "Taylor Swift Needs Fog Machines. God Does Not" in *Sojourners*, July 14, 2023. https://sojo.net/articles/taylor-swift-needs-fog-machines-god-does-not

made a request of God during the congregational prayer in a church, like in the Bible story about Hannah. My mother believes God answered that prayer.

For my people, church was not a choice or a luxury or something to enjoy. It was a place of fear and trembling about your soul. It was the "pillar and foundation of the truth" and was the place where people gave their lives to God, promptly and sincerely, as a "spiritual gift of worship." Our job was to offer ourselves up in humble thanks for salvation from sin and hell. If you wanted to meet God, you went, first and foremost, to church.

Preachers (back then, men only) were viewed as holy and set apart by God. A pastor's job from the pulpit was to be a conduit of God's mind and will, like water through a pipe. Often, in my denomination's churches, there was a plaque bolted to the pulpit which faced the pastor and quoted the Bible, "Sir, we would see Jesus."

My people lived their lives defined by a picture which was ubiquitous in the homes of our town. It was usually hanging on the wall above their dining room tables. In the picture, an old man with a white beard sat at his table, head bowed, weathered hands folded in prayer above a small crust of bread. It was a visible depiction of "Give us this day our daily bread" and of humble thanks to God. That picture hung in my grandparents dining room, too. It was the story of their life together: Simple and humble. The perimeter of the foundation of their one-story house was thirty-five-foot square. They prayed, they were nourished, they did their work for God. They went to church. They observed Sabbath.

With my people, if you didn't go to church twice on the Sabbath, your commitment to God was suspect. All the stores in my town were closed. Women peeled their Sunday dinner potatoes on Saturday and left them soaking in water overnight to reduce the amount of labor expended on the Lord's Day. Some of my forebears in dairy country would milk their cows on the Sabbath to ease the pain of the animals' bursting udders. Then the farmers poured the milk out into the ditches because they refused to profit from work done on the Lord's Day.

My mother's view of Sabbath explains how my people thought about God and life. When I was teenager, I complained to my mom about not being able to ride my bike or play basketball or watch T.V. on Sunday. Her response: "Well, when I think of all Jesus suffered for me, there is nothing He could ask me that I could say 'no' to."

It's tough to argue with that. People like my mom, in my denomination, taught me about Jesus and raised me in the faith.

For God's sake, the selling of alcohol was illegal in my town. Like most everybody else, though, my grandfather occasionally drove past the city limit sign and bought a small bottle. He kept it in a cupboard in the kitchen.

Simple **Faith**. Pure **Love**.

My people rose in the morning and, first thing, knelt to offer up their prayers, as if from an altar. Then, they stood up and did their work with diligence for God. From their pay, before any other expenditure, they calculated ten percent and devoted that to the Sunday morning offering plate. Those tithes supported missionaries, funded the seminary, and paid the pastor, in that order.

Marvel about this: At one church I served, an elderly couple, after they died, left a stunning financial gift to our church, and the same amount to nine other ministries. For years, whenever the two went out for coffee, they ordered one cup. They bowed to pray over it, and then split that one cup and each drank half, so they would have more to give to the Lord's work.

People with similar devotion prayed over my life. Preachers prayed for me because I was a baptized parishioner under their charge. Teachers at my Christian school prayed over me because I was their student. They fed my body and fed my soul and trained my mind and nurtured my life.

I'm certain that my boss, Jesse, from my first real job, prayed over me, too. Jesse operated a sewage truck. Day by day, he lowered himself into manholes, and scooped human waste from blocked sewage pipes with a small shovel. Years before that, though, when he was young, Jesse was a semi-pro baseball player, and was good enough to dream of the Big Leagues. That life, however, out on the road, brought Jesse

UnMediated

more temptation than he could handle: Jesse liked women, and they very much liked him. Jesse had a wife and small children. He prayed to God for guidance and then tried to think of a place where women wouldn't show up. To avoid sin, Jesse left his dream career and woke up every morning for the rest of his life to face one of dirtiest jobs in the world. Jesse did this for God. For a while, I was on Jesse's crew.

When I left my last church, I didn't just leave a job, or a salary, or a career. I left my people. Believers like my mom, my grandparents, and my boss, Jesse, populated my congregation. The church was only six miles away from my grandparents' house and from the sanctuary within which my mom had offered her prayer for a child. To this day, in my chaplaincy work, out of all the diverse people I visit, when I encounter someone from my heritage my heart floods with resonance and affection.

Broadly, though, these days, The Church as I knew it is no longer defined by the humble man bowing over his crust of bread. His great-grandkids, these days, nibble on Black Pepper Focaccia at Panera and sip Mocha Frappuccinos from Starbucks. They live in homes so large you could fit three or four of my grandparents' houses into them. They have extra houses in lakeside communities too, with golf carts tricked out with mag wheels, complete with little canvas garages for them.

The kids have become wealthy. Their forebears worked hard and prospered; the descendants got their share of the inheritance, tore down the small spaces, and built bigger ones. In my hometown, there is a brewery on Main Street, which is open seven days a week. In my conservative swath of West Michigan, we have now become champions of producing and mixing drinks. Our church buildings are laden with luxury. The members go out for brunch after the Sunday service. I understand. I like Sunday brunch, too. Truly, in this life, I also have received my good things.

From this position of power, wealth, and self-perceived righteousness, however, The Church seems to think it owns the world and can tell it what to do. It has lost its humility and turned into an entitled bully. Though most of us have situated our lives far from danger or human misery, somehow, it seems, we still feel threatened or persecuted. It appears Church people feel that they don't have enough and that they have been ripped off.

In the old days, however, when I was nineteen years old, I thought Jesus my Lord was commanding me to be a pastor. My mom, and my people, had shown me how not to refuse him. The following fall I enrolled at my denomination's college and then continued my ministerial studies at its seminary.

I would have been a pastor till I died, until the finest people I had known, who raised me and who had given me faith, succumbed all too easily to the hell-driven mindset of Donald Trump. I could not speak against him without losing my job. My first boss, Jesse, had shown me the way of Jesus: It's better

UnMediated

to lose your cushy, adulterous life than lose your soul.

I had to speak.

Jesus, Not Big Enough

In the spring of 2020, I preached a sermon, appealing for Christian unity. In our church, I said, there are a few beleaguered Christians who are Democrats. These Christian Democrats, I said, felt like they needed to be secretive about their views as they navigated the social dynamics of a much larger group of church members who were Republicans.

"Jesus is bigger than this," I said. My point was that we should be able, as brothers and sisters in faith, to speak about our political views without fear or shame. It's the essence of Christian unity to hold different views, and to know each other's perspectives, and still accept and honor one another.

The following week, I received a text from a Trump-supporting member of the congregation. The man said, "My wife and I will no longer be attending this church. We cannot attend a church where the senior pastor believes that a Democrat can be a Christian."

So. Jesus, not bigger, then.

The Elders, Suffering Me

In July of 2020, I sent a request to the elders of my church. By then, they had already suffered much to stand with me.

Simple **Faith**. Pure **Love**.

Two years earlier, two gay people, one of whom was a member of the church, got married. My wife, Alicia, and I believed they should be reckoned as believers. Alicia attended the wedding. At the behest of the elders, I did not.

The church suffered a nuclear explosion. A heat-frothed group of church members levied wrath upon Alicia and me, then left. Ever since, the church had been limping and bleeding. Two of the elders were taking heart meds to deal with the stress. Yet they loved me, and I loved them. Then, after all that pain, I presented them with a risky request.

I asked if they would allow me to speak publicly, outside our church walls, about my spiritual convictions regarding Donald Trump. I was thinking little things: A letter to the public editorial section of the local paper, perhaps, or speaking at small, out-of-town political gatherings.

Of course, I suggested, what I spoke outside of the walls of the church would leak back in. It would work out, I said. People knew me. I had been faithful at their hospital bedsides and at gravesides. Jesus is bigger than this.

The elders said "no." They said it respectfully and gently, but I suspect they were inwardly screaming, "Please, for God's sake, don't do this. We've suffered so much for you already. Please stop."

Un Mediated

The Text That Signaled the End

Two weeks after that gentle "no," I sent another request.

An organization called Vote Common Good, led by Doug Pagitt, was sponsoring a pastors' march from Charlottesville to Washington D.C. The pilgrimage was a proclamation against racism. I asked the elders if I could go. I said that I would use personal vacation time. If there was a photographer around, I would step away; if there was a reporter, I would be silent. In essence, I would take my convictions out of town. Weary as they must have been of me and, I suspect, glad to have a break from me, they said "yes."

Our pastor-group walked one hundred and thirty miles, ten to sixteen miles a day, on blistering hot highways. In Charlottesville, a local pastor met with us to describe what it was like in August of 2017 when the violence and vitriol of the KKK came to town. I stood in the spot where Heather Heyer was run over and killed by a white supremacist, and I listened to people who saw her die. During that walk, for the first time, I carried a Black Lives Matter sign.

Out on the highway, guys in trucks, even from way across the median, were sticking their arms out their windows, flipping us off, and screaming "Fuckin' idiots!" An old man glided past me in his car, muttering in his heavy drawl, with a hissing whisper, "Yeah, but *white lives matter more.*"

In the pictures from that walk, you can see me in the group photos, standing always in the back, wearing a large floppy hat, sunglasses, and a Covid-face mask. That was my disguise: Me, rolling in the dirt.

Throughout that pastor-trek, I was a spastic wreck. On long stretches of sunbaked pavement, the pastors patiently listened as I poured out my inner tension and sorrow. They recommended that when I got back, I settle down and keep doing the work of ministry. I was asking, "Shall I stay or shall I go?" These "liberal" pastors gently advised, "Stay."

I came home, knelt in the sanctuary, and told God "Yes" to that plan. I would shut-up and serve the people. I would preach well-behaved little sermons about Jesus, distribute the bread and juice, and visit the sick.

That lasted for two weeks, until a core member of my church, and one of my dearest friends there, confronted me with his views about Black Lives Matter. My mind was reeling. Did he know about the walk? If so, how? I tried to gently sidestep him, and to focus on our fellowship in Christ despite differing views.

Three weeks after that, like the reverberation of a funeral bell, came "The Text." He and his wife would no longer be attending our church. They could not attend a church where the senior pastor supports a "terrorist organization."

Which led to my final request.

In the Rain at Kitty Hawk

The "terrorist organization" text hit my phone on the Tuesday of a vacation in North Carolina.

UnMediated

The previous Saturday we had carried our luggage into our motel room through a rainstorm. We found some dried blood on the counter and dirt and grime everywhere else. We located another place and dragged our luggage to it through puddles. Monday morning, an infection erupted in one of my teeth. My face was aching and I couldn't find a dentist.

On that Tuesday morning, it had stopped downpouring for a few hours, so we took the chance to visit the beach. We were sitting in the wet sand when my phone beeped. I read the "terrorist organization" text, looked up from my phone, and said to Alicia, "Well, honey, it's over."

That evening, after swabbing my tooth with another dollop of topical pain killer, I emailed all the elders, requesting a meeting when I returned. I told them that there was no salve for this pain, and I would be initiating our denomination's formal church process for a pastor-church separation.

That week, Alicia and I wandered around Kitty Hawk in the drizzle wondering what to do next with my career.

The Church's Liars and Cheaters

My protest was not against my church. It was against the pit of shamefulness that The Church had become in the spiritual sway of Trumpism. The Church was abusing its pastors.

One pastor from my denomination was fired because, during Covid, he advocated for masks in worship services. Another was fired for reading the word "justice" from the prophet Isaiah. Church members and church *elders* from across our denomination were sending letters to denominational officials, laced with profanity and threats of physical violence.

In addition, some elders and deacons became cheaters. The leaders from one pastor's church were sneaking around in nighttime meetings, drawing up funky paperwork, trying to circumvent church policies and by-pass established denominational rules for the separation of churches and pastors.

Some elders and deacons from other churches became liars. They appeared before regional church bodies with trumped up statements and false reports of the failures of their pastors. They couldn't say out loud, "We are firing our pastor because we are locked in on Donald Trump's worldview, and we will accept no discussion or biblical critique of him or his policies." They were cowards, who knew exactly what they were doing and why, but would not openly admit their motivations. As they gave their hearts and minds to Donald Trump, many leaders in The Church became as small, dirty, and mean as he is.

I've heard Church-people try to deny it, but in the sway of their devotion to Donald Trump, they viscerally and palpably changed. They willfully exchanged the glory of their faith heritage for an earthly, toxic stew.

In my church, even throughout the separation, I was treated fairly and well. It didn't seem right to just sit on my hands, clamp my mouth shut, and watch these other pastors mistreated, while the governing bodies of the denomination put on sad faces, shrugged, and feigned helplessness. Pastors had no protection. No one stood for them.

At the same time, friends from around the country were telling me that something had changed in their churches. One said, "The conversations in the narthex after church turned dark." Another told of how, when people in his church figured out that he did not support Trump, they either argued with him or shunned him. He said, "People who had been my dearest friends for years were just *different*." Retired pastors with respected careers fell into depression, wondering what had happened to people they had served all their lives.

When I returned home from the terrorist-text-rain-toothache vacation, I met with the elders and described my belief that we should separate. My convictions were too deep, I said. I was miserable and so were they, and it would only get worse. Some of them wept and tried to convince me not to do this.

I loved them. They loved me. Yet I saw no other way.

My Unpardonable Sin

At the time, it wasn't my intention to bang the pulpit every Sunday and scream, "God says you may not support Donald Trump." It seemed to me, though, that on occasion, there should be a reasonable critique, just as there had always been of other presidents (Bill Clinton, for example). I had in mind the children and young people sitting in our sanctuary. It made no sense to read the Ten Commandments in church, and then, in the wake of another revelation of Trump's sinful behavior, be afraid to say, "Whatever you may think of the President, God is calling you to love and respect others. It is a sin to exploit people sexually. Racism is sin. It is against the will of God to lie and bully others. At the very least, Jesus calls us to compassion, kindness, and, yes, "justice."

Yet, even without using Donald Trump's name, if a pastor spoke about, for example, racism, church people got mad. Suddenly they were hot in the belief that there was no such thing in the world, and they viewed it as betrayal if a pastor suggested there was.

Pastors also ran into buzzards and buzzsaws because Churched Trumpers believed that no one needed to care about Covid – that it was somehow an offense against God and faith, or an attack on religion, to take reasonable precautions.

(After I left church ministry, I trained for chaplaincy in a hospital. Church people, while dying of Covid, spit and swore at the very hospital staff who were trying to save their lives. I blame Donald Trump's lies about Covid, and the pastors who preached Trump's lies as the will of God, for the needless, agonized deaths of those deluded people. Not to mention the abuse levied, in Jesus' name, against nurses and doctors. In my eyes, for the first time, Christianity manifested itself in that hospital, and broadly across America, as a type of mental illness. It still seems that way to me now.)

Somewhere in the swirl of the flying debris and mania of Religious Trumpism, a man from our church, one of our few, beleaguered Democrats, lamented, "*We* are the reason Donald Trump is in office. It's The *Church*. We put him there. We are responsible." His words rang like a bell in my heart.

My internal conviction became: "I only have a small voice. But what voice I have, I must use."

The last Sunday at my church was October 11, 2020. I decided that I had three weeks to raise my voice in confrontation against Religious Trumpism and to help get Donald Trump un-elected.

That's when I did what is considered in the world of Trump-Church the unpardonable sin, and it caused pain to the church I left: I spoke to a reporter.

Five Minutes of Fame

On our local paper's website, there was a mailbox for questions and comments. I clicked on it. I wrote that I was a pastor leaving my church to confront Religious Trumpism. Three days later, a reporter called, and we met for an interview. I thought, if anything, it would be a small piece in the religion section. I thought it would be a local, hometown discussion.

It was bigger than that. The story made it into national newspapers. For a while, it was a whirlwind.

People from around the country, and sometimes overseas, emailed or sent online messages. Alicia and

Simple **Faith**. Pure **Love**.

I read them all and wept. We heard spiritual pain. Beaten under the hand of Trumpist churches, people poured out their stories of spiritual lostness. Pastors shared their anguish. One man even showed up at our door, in his work clothes, hands in his pockets, and tears in his eyes. He said, "I've been here four times today, hoping to find you. I just wanted to say thank you."

Un Mediated

Simple **Faith**. Pure **Love**.

SECTION TWO
Ninety-Foot Statue
Exactly Why I Oppose Religious Trumpism

Un Mediated

The Core of It

It is this: A large portion of The Church attaches the name and cause of Jesus to Donald Trump. The rest of The Church appeases this sacrilege.

The Church has abandoned the Gospel and has lost the heart and message of Jesus.

A pastor should speak about that.

The Bible tells a story: A king erected a ninety-foot golden statue. The national leaders issued a command that when the band plays, all the people must bow to the statue. The command came with a threat: Bow down with everybody else or be thrown into a blazing furnace of fire. Think of the ego of a king who would commission such a statue and issue such a threat.

Donald Trump demands complete loyalty and deals in threats and fear. As the world witnessed on January 6, 2021, he stimulated violence for the sake of his own vainglory. He fanned the flames of human conflict for his name's sake, and, when that violence erupted, he enjoyed the spectacle.[7]

7- For descriptions of Trump's enjoyment of January 6, see Patricia Zengerle and Richard Cowan, "Trump Watched Jan. 6 U.S. Capitol Riot Unfold on TV, Ignored Pleas to Call for Peace" in *Reuters*, July 22, 2022. *https://www.reuters.com/world/us/us-capitol-probes-season-finale-focus-trump-supporters-three-hour-rage-2022-07-21/*
Also see Peter Wade, "'Look at All Those People Fighting for Me': Trump 'Gleefully' watched Jan. 6 Riot, Says Former Press Secretary" in *Rolling Stone*, January 6, 2022. *https://www.rollingstone.com/politics/politics-news/stephanie-grisham-trump-gleefully-watched-jan-6-1280113/*

Simple **Faith**. Pure **Love**.

The leaders who surround him, some of them nationwide pastors, tell Christians they must bow down and follow along. Most of them are doing so.

I view this as idolatry. I will not bow.

The Answer When the Elder Asked, "Why?"

When I met with the elders to suggest we separate, one of them said, "So let's say you do this. Then what? Trump gets elected, or Biden does. What becomes of you then? You won't have a job. You won't be able to preach. What will you have left?"

I said, "My conscience."

The Bible tells the story of Jeremiah, yelling at God about the misery of being a prophet. In essence, Jeremiah says to God, "You lied to me. You called me to be a prophet, and I thought this would be a fulfilling life. Instead, everybody hates me."

Jeremiah continues: "But if I say, 'I will not mention God, or speak anymore in God's name,' then God's word is in my heart like a fire—a fire shut up in my bones. I am weary of holding it in; indeed, I cannot."

That's how I felt.

My soul was troubled from the time Donald Trump came down the escalator to announce his first campaign. Then, when 81% of the white American Evangelical Church became his core support, I felt something splitting within me.

Able to say nothing without wrecking the church I loved, I remember walking through the church sanctuary in the early morning darkness, anguished, weary and empty. I remember thinking: "This is going to kill me. I am going to die this way." It seemed to me, in those moments, like a pathetic way to live and die.

I had to speak.

Answer to the Denominational Official

I wrote a public article explaining why I left my denomination. One of its officials asked to meet for coffee.

He was friendly and kind. He kept asking, though, "Why? Why would you write something like this? Back at the office, we're all wondering why you would do that to us?"

My answer is: This is about the Gospel.

People feel that I betrayed them. Yet this is about what Jesus told us about God. This is about what God thinks about people, and about how Jesus wants us to be in relation to other human beings. This is about how a person finds peace with God.

I couldn't shake the conviction that The Church did not reflect the heart of God in answer to those questions.

What the African Refugee Said

In Lille, France, in 2017, I volunteered with The International Association for Refugees. I met kids as young as fourteen years old, who had been younger still when they crossed deserts and oceans to flee Africa. Most of them had been beaten, robbed, and raped on the way. When they had arrived in Lille, the people of the town welcomed them and took turns, four families to one refugee, housing and feeding them.

One of these young men summarized for me the message of Donald Trump: "He puffs out his chest and tells me there is no hope for me."

People ask me why I set my career on fire. I did it for that kid, and everyone like him in the world. I did it to oppose The Church, which enthusiastically joins Donald Trump as a bullying force, and which in so doing employs the name and imagery of Jesus to hurt, harm, and endanger the weakest and poorest among us.

Examples of The Church's Trump Worship

It is inexplicable to me how a church, or a pastor, or any Christian can avoid explicitly setting itself apart examples like these of the idolatry of Religious Trumpism:

- In 2021, some Church people in Georgia erected a billboard. It quoted the Bible, regarding the birth of Jesus: "For unto us a child is born; unto us a Son is given." The billboard displayed, under the quote, a picture of Donald Trump.[8]

8- For more on the billboard "A Son is Given," see Jack Beresford, "Billboard Comparing Donald Trump to Jesus Christ Removed" in *Newsweek*, September 15, 2021. *https://www.newsweek.com/billboard-comparing-donald-trump-jesus-christ-removed-georgia-1629381*

Un Mediated

- The "Christian" people who stormed the Capitol and attacked police officers at Trump's behest on January 6, 2021 proclaimed God as their motivation. They carried Trump flags and crosses, and portrayed Jesus in a MAGA hat.[9]

- As I write this paragraph, it is Holy Week of 2024. As Donald Trump entered a courtroom to face charges of paying hush money to a porn star, he celebrated and embraced the writings of one of his followers, who had compared Trump's legal sufferings to those of Jesus.[10]

9- For a sampling of Christian imagery at the Capitol on January 6, 2021, see Tyler Merbler's photograph "MAGA Jesus" on *Uncivil Religion*, January 6, 2021. *https://uncivilreligion.org/home/media/maga-jesus*

Gina Ciliberto and Stephanie Russell-Kraft, "They Invaded the Capitol Saying 'Jesus Is My Savior. Trump Is My President'" in *Sojourners*, January 7, 2021, *https://sojo.net/articles/they-invaded-capitol-saying-jesus-my-savior-trump-my-president*

Jack Jenkins, "Police Officer Says Capitol Rioters 'Perceived Themselves to Be Christians'" in *The Roys Report*, July 27, 2021 *https://julieroys.com/capitol-rioters-perceived-themselves-christians/*

10- For comparisons of Trump's sufferings to those of Jesus, see Andrew Stanton, "Donald Trump Shares Jesus Comparison While in Court" in *Newsweek*, March 25, 2024. *https://www.newsweek.com/donald-trump-shares-jesus-comparison-while-court-stormy-daniels-1883109*

Church members have said to me, "Well that's not *us*. We don't believe or do stuff like that." Yet no pastor in my denomination or in the larger Church world could stand up and *say that* from a pulpit. No pastor could speak a rational, biblical, or theological word in response to this bizarre, idolatrous, vicious, fantasy religion without losing their jobs.

I concluded that if a church cannot and will not do the hard work of describing the message of God for humanity in contrast to Religious Trumpism, or for that matter any earthly power systems, it is a wasted enterprise. People claiming to know God and possess "The Truth" had enslaved themselves and the message of God to an evil, hell-driven person, though they had many other more righteous (by The Church's standards) candidates from which to choose.

Church people think the country is in moral decline. I don't disagree. But if we can't transform a culture by embodying the heart and mindset of Jesus, then we have left his realm and have abandoned his influence. As Jesus said, we have become like salt with no saltiness. As the Apostle said, we are fighting a war with weapons that are not God's. We got nuthin'.

A Church in Dementia

In my current role as a hospice chaplain, I visit a woman suffering dementia. In my presence, the woman looked at her daughter, Willow, and said, "If I could do it again, I wouldn't give birth to you."

Which leaves Willow wounded and wondering: "Is that the dementia talking? Or is it some awful, latent truth, which has been smoldering in my mother's heart for fifty-five years?" People like Willow never know for sure. Yet every day, Willow must return to care for her mother. I believe The Church, the spiritual mother who formed me, nurtured me, and blessed me, has lost its mind. In its dementia, it is using God's name to give religious adulation to a man whose every imagination is evil. She attends his rallies and applauds his cruel, racist, and violent views and actions. I now believe those views and attitudes were always latent within The Church, and within me.

In addition, in its dementia, The Church is saying to many of its baptized children (LGBTQ+ persons): "I don't want you." And it is saying to Indigenous people, African American people, Asian People, Hispanic people, people of other nationalities and backgrounds, "We don't see you. If someone, including the President of the United States, slanders, denigrates, or threatens you, we will do nothing and say nothing. We will not stand with you or for you."

Trump's words, behaviors, and attitudes are antithetical to Jesus. Yet, as musician Dan Deitrich wrote to The Church, "All I heard was silence, or worse you justified it. You baptized it with language torn from the pages of the Good Book."[11]

11- For Dan Deitrich's song to The Church, see "Hymn for the 81%." YouTube, uploaded by Daniel Deitrich, 28 September 2022, *https://www.youtube.com/watch?v=WidUnxxovD8*

Simple **Faith**. Pure **Love**.

The duty of Willow's love requires her to go back and tend to her mom.

I abandoned my spiritual Mother. I walked away, sad for the loss of her.

Lament

The Church. What, then, shall I say about it?

It had it all, it seemed to me.

It had a theology of peace with God. It had the message of Jesus. It taught that the purpose of life is to glorify God in every word and deed. It taught me to offer my life to God, promptly and sincerely. It gave me everything.

It had the moral foundation for living. A person could follow its teachings and live a successful life.

It formed and molded some of the most beautiful, courageous, and generous people I have known, many of whom became mentors and benefactors in my life.

It had work ethic. My forebears came to America as immigrants and started with nothing. They took the lowest jobs—in muck farms, or in the garbage business. With prayer, and by the sheer sweat of their brows, they worked their way into well-stewarded prosperity.

I believed The Church was the hope of the world.

Now, with its heart and mind astray, I believe The Church is becoming bad, even dangerous, for the world. I have lost faith The Church and in its mes-

Un Mediated

sage. In my mind and soul, I cannot make it work anymore.

I love you. I'm sorry. I cannot stay.

Summary of Section Two:

I tell you this to describe, from my own experience, why I believe something is spiritually and catastrophically wrong in The Church in North America. The Church has changed. My perception of it has, too. In our time, it is not to be trusted with God's message for your soul. It is spiritually and physically dangerous.

Later, I would like to offer a way, simple and pure, to find God and experience Jesus, unmediated by The Church. Before that, I should explain that my own heart and mind began to change prior to the arrival of Donald Trump on the political scene, and five years before I clicked on the newspaper's website.

UnMediated

Simple **Faith**. Pure **Love**.

UnMediated

Simple **Faith**. Pure **Love**.

SECTION THREE

Stones in the Windshield

*Prior Events Which Began to Weaken
My Faith in The Church*

UnMediated

You know how it is: A stone from the highway smacks into the windshield of your car. That stone may be small, leaving only a tiny crack in the glass. Over time, however, that crack creeps across the glass in jagged lines until everything shatters.

People at my last church would not be wrong to wonder: "What happened? We hired this nice pastor. Then he went wild."

I didn't expect it either. Long before I arrived at my last church, however, and before Trump came down the escalator, there had been these two stones. . . .

These two experiences had to do with the issue of human sexuality. Without question, that issue was a factor in my emerging spiritual trouble with The Church and its teachings.

The Man Who Couldn't Speak

Years earlier, at a previous church, a man visited a Sunday service. After the service, one of the man's friends asked, on his behalf, if he could meet with me.

The man was in a suit and tie, a formality which was rare in our congregation. We made introductions, but small talk was difficult. The man's face was tight. He was having a difficult time swallowing. I went to get him a glass of water.

He was sweating. Then he leaned forward, rested his elbows on his knees, and just hung there, like a scarecrow after the ropes which had been holding its body upright have come loose.

Simple **Faith**. Pure **Love**.

Agonized silence.

After twenty minutes of misery, I asked if he would simply want to pray. He nodded, and I placed my hand on him and blessed him. We parted gently. He never did find any words. Two years later his friend told me that the man was gay. I would've been the first person he told, and he just couldn't do it.

The spiritual torment of that man altered me. My heart became effaced. Whatever might have been the barriers of religious principle or bias within me, those barriers became increasingly thin, until nonexistent. In that moment, I could not imagine anything other than God's full and unconditional love for him. I felt such love within myself.

This man, long before the rise of Donald Trump, caused me to question my foundational views about my Christianity. In seminary, my favorite class was called "The Doctrine of Humanity and Salvation." I cherish it still. Deep within me, however, after the meeting with the agonized man, I began to suspect that my personal view of humanity was too small, and my doctrine of salvation too narrow, as compared with the effaced heart of God.

The experience with that man was like a stone that, after years of time, began to shatter my soul. It wasn't my last church's fault that my way of thinking and believing fell apart while I was their pastor.

Un Mediated

When Alicia Confronted the School Board

If you go by what her tormentors say, this whole thing is my wife Alicia's fault. I am proud to say they are not entirely wrong. My heart began to change after Alicia had the courage to stand up against a hypocritical Christian school board on behalf of one child. What she suffered there was the second stone in my windshield.

Back in 2014, we were living in Northern Michigan. I was pastoring a happy church. Alicia was, and still is, a respected and sought after professional counselor. We lived in a beautiful home, which our church had helped us build. Life was in a sweet spot.

We sent our kids to the local Christian school. Alicia was always volunteering there and eventually was elected to serve on its board. She was appointed Secretary of the Board and was therefore automatically on the Executive Committee.

I remember the night when she came home from a board meeting. I heard the door slam, and I heard Alicia's car keys scrape against our countertop. I came down the hallway from the back of the house, and my first glimpse of my wife was of her leaning against the counter, her hands gripping the edge of it. Her head was hanging down. Her shoulders were shaking. She was breathing heavily and weeping.

During Alicia's second year on the board, an alumnus of the school had enrolled a child in preschool. By the policy of the school, *anybody* can be in the preschool program. If, however, your child was kindergarten age or above, you had to quantify your faith and show proof of your doctrine and life, were required to fill out forms validating that you were an active church member and had to provide a pastor's recommendation. Pre-school, though, for the sake of getting prospective families in the door, was open for anyone, no stipulations. It was a marketing thing. All a kid needed was warm blood and a beating heart.

Except that this one child's parents were a same-sex, married couple.

The board, in direct violation their own written policy, to this child, said, "No." They did it behind closed doors. They did it with snide condemnations. One board member said, "God created Adam and Eve, not Adam and Steve." After that meeting, as Alicia was holding onto our countertop, she kept saying, between sobs, "They were mean. They were just so mean. . . ."

I tell you this: You can trust Alicia. If you're human, and suffering, she will be with you, and stand for you.

Alicia wrote a letter of protest and read it aloud at the next board meeting. She requested for her letter to be recorded in the minutes. (Two other board members came to her later and told her that they agreed with her and respected her. Alicia, however, is the one who *spoke*.)

After she read the letter, Alicia was shunned by the other board members. Though, as Secretary, she was

UnMediated

an officer on the Executive Committee, the other Exec members held meetings without inviting her. Ultimately, Alicia wrote a second letter, this one of resignation from the board. She had concluded that she could not in good conscience serve with the board and would not be a part of implementing its hypocrisy.

In her resignation, Alicia offered to stay for one or two months to help wrap up details and ensure a smooth transition. The board president, however, said, "No, you can leave *now*." Alicia gathered her papers and left the boardroom, with the other members' hot daggers in her back, and with their complicit silence slamming the door behind her.

I have since concluded that Alicia's job in God's world is to do what's right and get shit on for it. At the last church I served, after Alicia had attended the same-sex wedding, a vicious group of church people slandered her, gossiped against her, gave her the cold shoulder, and made her the target of their religious venom.

Despite those attacks, a number of people from our last church reached out and loved Alicia well. A larger group stood aside, looked askance, and kept their distance. There was no way of knowing who to trust. For Alicia, it felt like nowhere was safe.

Yet every Sunday, she walked up to the front doors of the church, said a prayer, took a breath, and went in. Alicia kept her dignity, held her head high, and faced the vicissitudes of the narthex crowd alone.

Alone, because I was always somewhere else in the building, getting the last-minute prep-work done on my obedient, tidy little sermons. I was rushing around, doing my pastoral glad-handing, rolling in the dirt for one more Sunday.

The school board, though: That was the Second Stone. More than we knew at the time, what the Christian school board did fractured not only Alicia's heart, but mine. It was spiritually consequential. It revealed, for me, what was brewing underneath the heart of The Church.

The whole experience was the beginning of a long road to leaving the Christianity which had raised me.

A little over a year after the incident with the school board, I interviewed for my last church. People told me about the gay couple attending the church, and they seemed to speak of it as an example of the congregation's welcoming heart. It seemed like the congregation had an openness that matched mine. I took the job.

The spiritual cracks were spreading within my heart, then, even before Donald Trump ran for president. As time went on, though, and as The Church in America gave its heart to Trump, I increasingly felt, in my shattered bones, that it was losing connection with the message of Jesus for humanity.

I began at pastoring my last church two months after Donald Trump began his first term as president. It was a collision neither the church nor I wanted or expected.

UnMediated

We, the Stone-Shattered

I'm thinking now that, over my years as a pastor, I had encountered many people who, somewhere in their past, had been smacked by a stone.

They were cordial but kept their distance. They showed up, maybe, for Christmas and Easter, or for a grandmother's funeral, or a children's program. When these folks showed up, they were polite, but exited quickly.

I judged that maybe they were lazy or hard-hearted. Now I wonder how many were just stone shattered. Maybe they had suffered a tragedy. Maybe God had coldly refused to answer a fervent and holy prayer. Maybe a church had failed them and they never recovered. For example, one young man who avoided church confided in me that when he was a child the other kids in Sunday School had bullied him. He never could, for the rest of his life, stomach being in a sanctuary.

With such folks, I kept imagining that if I preached in a compelling or convicting way, or if I proved myself to be a really, *really*, nice pastor-person, they would awaken to God and become active Christians. Now, I am embarrassed by that kind of thinking.

If you feel lost about God and church, you are not lazy or crazy. You're not a spiritual failure. I am sorry I ever thought that way.

Sometimes, there are just too many cracks.

We are the stone-shattered.

Simple **Faith**. Pure **Love**.

You are Not Alone

Jack, a friend of a friend, texted me. He said, "Lynn and I are currently not part of a church. It has been a bit of a struggle. We just had a baby, though. We still want to do a dedication for our son. Would this be something you are willing to do? Just a small ceremony, with family, in our backyard."

Lynn and Jack were born and raised in The Church. As adults they have been committed members. The "bit of a struggle," however, is that the era of Covid and of Religious Trumpism revealed The Church's heart. The Church's rejection of gay or trans persons revealed its heart, too. Lynn and Jack have weighed and measured The Church and concluded that it lacks credibility about God, humanity, and life. They don't want to raise their child in it.

Or consider my friend Art. He is smart, funny, and has been a committed Christian and leader in his congregation for his whole adult life. Every week for twenty years he has met with a group of men from his church for theological discussion. Most of the men in the group have become Trump supporters. Art texted me to say: "I told the group that if I wasn't already a Christian, I doubt if I would become one in light of who and what I see them prioritizing. It got quiet. No excommunication yet."

My friend Laurie, a lifelong Christian and committed churchgoer, texted: "I struggle the most with family and friends who continue to profess to be Christians, but spout the hate and violence which are

UnMediated

so indicative of Trump. When I see church signs and hear Christian music, it makes my blood pressure go up. I need to concentrate to remember that not all the people who grace those buildings or listen to that type of music are bad people."

If you get online and type the question, "Are people leaving The Church?" you will find varying statistics, but any way you cut it, it's a lot of people. While you are searching through the articles, you will find many opinions as to why.

Lynn and Jack, Art, and Laurie – and many others I have met - have sensed the lameness and the danger of The Church in our day.

That's why.

If you have sensed this too, if you are shattered, know this: You are not alone.

Un Mediated

Simple **Faith**. Pure **Love**.

UnMediated

Simple **Faith**. Pure **Love**.

SECTION FOUR
Rebuilding at Sixty
Career and Religion Change

UnMediated

You Will Suffer Loss

My last day at the church was October 11, 2020. That same month, I began as an unpaid chaplain intern at a mental health hospital, where I worked on the suicide unit through the spring of 2021. The following fall I began working as a resident chaplain at a Tier One hospital, 75 minutes from our house. It paid a stipend and provided health insurance.

It was just enough. We stripped our budget. Alicia's career carried us (and still does). It was tight, but we were never even close to destitute. Still, I worried a lot about our future.

Over the course of the year-long residency at the hospital, one night and day at a time, I drove 35,000 miles, working twelve-hour and twenty-four-hour shifts. I took classes and wrote papers. Then, in those hospital rooms and Emergency Department trauma bays, I encountered human chaos and suffering at a faster pace and at a grittier level that at any other time in my sheltered life.

On purpose, I lost thirty pounds. It was a time to get leaner and walk lighter. If I ever got a job interview, I was hoping to look younger than I was.

During that year, I also took shifts as an on-call chaplain at our local hospital. Simultaneously, I transitioned my ordination from my previous denomination to the United Church of Christ. More class time. More books to read. More papers to write.

You can tell that I feel proud of myself. Yes, I do. When I began this transition, I was sixty years old. By nature, I like safety and security. Change makes me anxious. Suddenly, I felt like a plastic grocery bag in a windstorm. Yet I had to find a new career, a new life, a new faith, and a new way of being.

Maybe you don't have to find a new career. If, however, God is calling your soul away from your old, toxic faith and into a new way of being, know this: You need to choose it. It's going to hurt. It will require that you abandon old patterns, dispose of previously precious religious habits, and forsake the opinions, and possibly the friendships, of people you love. You will have to make clear decisions. You will have to suffer loss.

For me it was grueling. It was frightening. I highly recommend it.

I recommend it because in the suffering of the suicide unit and in the chaos of those hospital trauma bays, in the books I read and in the classes I took, I stumbled upon the very smallest signs of God. Small as those signs were, they sustained my soul. They were all I had, because through it all I felt so very lost. I still feel that way, even now. I should explain that feeling, not to whine or complain about it, but so that perhaps you can feel some comfort and companionship there.

UnMediated

Simple **Faith**. Pure **Love**.

SECTION FIVE
Soul in a Snowy Ditch
What It Felt Like to be Spiritually Lost

Un Mediated

An Awful Conclusion About My Life

Even now, I don't know what to think of my career as a pastor. Some people think I was the worst pastor they ever knew, and I cannot fault them. It is true: I blew it sometimes. I have my share of failures. Worst of all, as I see it now, I sometimes preached with brimstone in my throat about subjects like drunkenness and sexual sin. Not to mention all that rolling in the dirt.

Amazingly, other people, with heartfelt thankfulness, tell me that when I was their pastor, I blessed them, and was for them the instrument of God I prayed to be.

Of one thing I am certain: I gave it my whole heart. In the darkness of many weekday mornings, I laid facedown down on the sanctuary floor to pray. On Sunday mornings, with my guts flat on the carpet, I told God that I would not stand up on that platform to preach until I had been down here on the floor talking to him. Other times I prayed while walking on gravel roads and in forests. Once, I fasted for seven days, culminating with the Sunday sermon. One Christmas Eve I left my family to visit someone in life-crisis. On many occasions, I set my alarm for three or four o'clock in the morning and drove two hundred miles to a hospital, so that I could pray with a church member before their surgery.

My mantra is: Pray your heart out; work your butt off. In ministry, that's what I did. I cared, with my whole self, for God and the church. I tried so very hard.

That's what I would have told you about my life and ministry before all of this.

However, three months into the internship at the mental health hospital, I told my peer group: "I'm sixty years old. I think I've wasted my life."

I Became a Person Without Faith

For all my previous life and ministry, I had no doubt there was sin in the church, because, for one thing, I was present within it. Though fully a fallen person, I was embraced by The Church, and loved. I ate and drank the sacrament.

There was no doubt also because there were other sinners like me, in abundance. As a pastor, I had a front row seat to religious failure and catastrophe everywhere. People, in my office, or in their living rooms, either revealed their own sin or collapsed, weeping, telling about the sins of their spouses or their kids. On occasion I collected guns from the homes of congregation members who were abusive or violent. I visited my members in jail and kept their secrets. One church required that I review the background checks of members who volunteered for children's ministry. The reports were a little shocking sometimes, but with assurances that it was all in the past, I signed the volunteer waivers.

Sin in the church, however, never took me to the point of spiritual departure. It never broke me.

What sustained me, for one thing, was the presence of so many Christians who exhibited the beauty of God, even while humbly admitting their fallen condition. Through the witness of their lives, I was

Un Mediated

sustained by the message of grace, of the kind Philip Yancey described. He told the story of Will Campbell, who, when challenged to define the Christian message in ten words or less, said: "We're all bastards, but God loves us anyway."[12] As Yancey tells the agonizing story, Campbell was brutally tested in that definition, yet retained his faith. There came a day, though, when I could not. Sin in The Church finally broke me.

Since I viewed the "81%" as having a sinful attachment to Donald Trump; I lost my faith in the entire project of The Church and in its message. It's like going to a tree, looking for fruit, and finding none. It's like fall harvest in an orchard when you discover the apples have sprouted piranha teeth. If this was the fruit of The Church, I decided, then the very root of its "Gospel" is vicious.

To the degree that I still believed in God, and in Jesus, it was a cognitive, abstract belief. I had no spiritual nerve endings, no feelings of faith. I was completely numb.

Even now, I have no desire for a corporate "worship" experience and no trust in human messages about God. Allow me to illustrate this: In my work as a chaplain, I visit nursing facilities. Each patient's room, of course, has a T.V. Since most of the people are partially deaf, their televisions are set at ear-splitting levels. Some of the facility patients are watching

---

12- See Philip Yancey, *What's So Amazing About Grace?* Zondervan 1997, 142.

church services. As I walk through the hallways I can hear the preachers, and sometimes catch glimpses of them on the screens.

At the same time, from other rooms, come the sounds and sights of soap operas, Hallmark romances, T.V. courtrooms and judges, commercials pitching the perfect deodorants and underwear, and sitcom reruns with their laugh tracks. Here is my condition: As I journey through the facilities, the messages echo and blend in the hallways. The preacher people and the romantic actor people and the fake audience laughter and the deodorant and underwear people all morph into one; it all looks and sounds like the same stuff and substance to me.

In former days, I listened to Christian music all the time. Now, I feel a vomitous reflex for anything with a fish sticker and a tune.

Strange to say: I believe in God, but I am a person without faith. I have no feeling for, nor any trust in, humanly generated messages about divine things.

It's been this way for a quite a while now.

The Confounding Mystery of Jason's Faith

Many people have far greater cause to lose faith than I have.

For example, I visit Jason, a fifty-two-year-old man who was a construction worker. He has a wife and four kids. Five years ago, Jason was in an accident. His brain swelled. He underwent a surgery which

Un Mediated

was only partially successful. Now he lives in a wheelchair, in a care facility, surrounded by people thirty years older than he, who suffer dementia. Jason's limbs don't work well, his head cannot remain upright sometimes, and his mouth can only form intelligible words half the time. He insists on feeding himself, but the food ends up smeared all over his face and body.

All day long, Jason listens from his phone to hyper-conservative preachers. He is trying to complete an online course from those same preachers, hoping to become one himself.

After we talk together, as I rest my hand on his shoulder to pray, Jason slowly, painstakingly forms words. He says to me, "I . . . have . . . a lifelong . . . disability, but . . . the Lord . . . gets me . . . through."

Stricken by the beauty of him, I face the mystery: The messages of those toxic preachers sustain Jason. Their sermons mediate the strength of God to him. The religion that upholds Jason is like the religion that formed and sustained me for most of my life.

All I can say is: Now it doesn't. When I enter Jason's room, the words of the sermons blaring out from his phone are repulsive to me.

Messages are blaring from within my own soul, too. Those messages are the voices from my spiritual past, telling me that I am rebelling, that my heart is hard, and that I need to repent. "You just need faith!" the voices say.

You might as well say to a punctured balloon, "Inflate thyself."

I have no defense. There is no explanation. I know this hurts and offends people I love. I cannot understand it, nor can I fix it. My previous faith is gone. My only hope, as I will soon share: These days I meet God elsewhere.

Feeling Like A Nuthin'

The newspaper articles went public. I either had initiated them or consented to them. For a while, Alicia and I lived in a whirlwind. I had made those decisions and those choices, but I did not expect to feel so lost in the storm that followed.

Prayer didn't work anymore. I got down on my face, like before, and found only cold floor. As in my former spiritual practice, I walked in the breeze of early morning, birds singing all around, and was unmoved. I had no words.

I tried attending a church. That's what you're supposed to do if you want to find God, right? I went to a trusted and beloved friend, who pastored a small local congregation. He was, as always, good to me. The members of his church, even knowing who I was and what I had done, welcomed me tenderly. It was not their fault that I sat among them as a corpse. Eventually, I apologized to my friend and stopped attending. I didn't have the strength to pretend.

As for The Church, large and in charge? The whole project looked to me as something vapid and stupid, "a tale told by an idiot, full of sound and fury, signifying nothing." In a low valley, I concluded that for thirty years I had been an idiot telling that tale.

When my kids were little, we watched *Winnie the Pooh* videos together. In one episode, Tigger takes a bath. He pops out to find that his stripes have washed away in the suds. He spends the episode trying to find himself, and finally, alone, he slumps away muttering, "What is a guy, when he's a nuthin'?"

That was me. I lost the markers of my faith, and my identity.

How ironic. I did this all for God and promptly lost all divine sensation. This hardly seemed fair.

Leave The Place Where Jesus Is Not

In my deepest time of lostness, I had no answers for anything. Nor did I have clear explanations. I prayed for guidance and found none.

All I had was this: I thought I could feel, in my heart, *where Jesus wasn't*.

That was enough.

It's like having a bee allergy. If you hear buzzing, then you run, to anywhere else, fast. Spiritually, I had no clear direction. I just knew what I had to get away from.

I would like to offer this: You don't have to know what your ultimate plan is. You don't need to know how it will turn out. But if your soul knows that what you're hanging onto, the religion you are clinging to, is not Jesus, then get away from it fast, with all your might, to anywhere else. Push away, hard, from its superficial comforts, and keep walking.

God Will Send You People

It's easy to say, "just get out of there." It's awful, though. You are making yourself an outcast. It's like high school, when you make a choice to leave a friend group, and now you must enter the cafeteria, alone, with your lunch tray. You look across a sea of people, and no one smiles or motions to you to come over. You must sit by yourself.

In my case, God cushioned me. The very instant I left, I entered chaplaincy training, which meant that I was assigned to peer-learning groups. To those dear folks, I poured out my soul. They listened to me and loved me.

Also, I met with Dr. Bert Van Hoek every two weeks. He is a professional counselor and mentor. Bert was like a father to me.

Then, smack in the middle of the whirlwind, one couple reached out to us, scooped us up, and swept us away on a weekend to their home in Colorado. We were on shaky legs; they steadied us and showered love upon us.

Also, Alicia and I encountered pastor-couples we had not known before, who became dear and trusted companions.

In our case, it was all miraculous.

Un Mediated

If you "get yourself out of there," I cannot promise you will have it so good. If I may offer a few ideas about this:

First, we allowed ourselves to take a break. For a time, we didn't go anywhere on Sunday mornings. We rested on the Sabbath Day. We didn't force anything in terms of church. We let ourselves be alone. For a time, "Sabbath alone" gave us space to heal.

Second, in my case, I purposefully stepped away from previous relationships. I had strong relationship people at my last church, and I had to close those doors, for my sake, and for the church's sake. This was difficult, and it hurt people's feelings. But it had to be done.

Third, Alicia and I intentionally opened ourselves to new things. If someone new asked us to get together, we smiled and said "yes."

My friend Richard said something helpful and hopeful. He's a retired pastor. He and his wife Ruth "got out of there." I asked him if it was hard.

"Oh, yes, terribly hard," he said. "We lost a lot of friends." I asked him how he handled that.

Richard smiled and said, "We made a lot of new ones."

For a short while, you may have to stand there, bereft, an empty tray in your hand, feeling vulnerable. It may take some time, but I do believe things will turn around.

You will never know, however, the joy of those new relationships unless you shear yourself away from the old ones.

In our case, we fell into the arms of the United Church of Christ. Later, at the very end of this book, I will tell you about that – about what the pastor who was being harassed and threatened by Trump followers said which touched me like a butterfly, and about the panel discussion which made my eyes well up with tears.

What I Don't Do about Lostness

I have decided, for myself, and with regard to other people, not to try and fix lostness, or resist it, panic about it, or allow guilt about it.

When we lived in Northern Michigan, during heavy snowstorms, when all the schools and businesses were closed, young guys would get out their four-wheel drive pick-up trucks and take turns driving as hard and fast as they could into ditches and fields. Then they took out their tow straps and yanked each other out. Just for fun.

I have decided to let my soul rest in the ditch. If God has a tow strap, let God come use it.

I've always had the sense that at all costs you must build a fortress against Lostness. Then my own walls crumbled.

The Christian answer is to *fix it*. Go to a church! Listen to a sermon! Desperately inundate your mind with Christian content. Listen to Christian music, all day, and even during the night. Read a Christian book. Reach up! Climb out! *Believe!* And if not that,

UnMediated

then at least pretend so that you can fit in.

I won't. I have given up on *trying really hard*. I will not lie to God. I will not roll in the dirt of human religious expectation. I will accept no merely human answers or reasoning. I have no space within me and no shred of patience for man-made religious fantasy-systems. Maybe someday my trust will come back. For now, it is gone.

I want God, and God alone, to tow me out. That or nothing.

You're expecting me to say, "And God did! Look at me now! I attend a church! I was lost, but now I'm found!"

No. It's not like that at all. True, I am a pastor. Yes, I sit in a gathering on Sunday mornings. Occasionally, I even offer sermons. My faith, though, in terms of punctuation, is a question mark. I talk to God from a perpetual snowy ditch.

Sometimes, though, I feel the slightest tugging sensations. Ironically, it very much involves humans. Since those tugging sensations now form the simple core of my faith, I'd like to tell you about that.

Un Mediated

Simple **Faith**. Pure **Love**.

UnMediated

Simple **Faith**. Pure **Love**.

SECTION **SIX**

Friends in Forsaken Places

Where, Sometimes, I Encounter Jesus

Un Mediated

God Tugs at me Through People.

Not people standing on platforms or speaking from behind pulpits. Not people singing in a sanctuary. I feel the pull of the divine when I meet with human beings who have been cast down into forsaken places.

This is my ragged trinity:

> I meet God in people who are suffering and who are in weakness.
>
> I meet Jesus in human compassion.
>
> I feel the Spirit breathing through nearly-dead people.

I would like to share how this happens, at least for me. After that, I would like to express how this has reshaped my core theology.

God In Nearly-Dead People

I find God in breathing corpses. No one can manufacture this. Nobody is attracted to this. Shining spotlights on the nearly-dead person through fog-machine smoke will not attract a crowd.

Freda, for example. You can see her bones through her skin. She has been skeletal for over a year, and she just won't die. She lays there, all day, every day, in her bed, pulling her knees up, and sliding them back down. Sometimes she calls out "Bup-bup-bup-bup-bup-bup." Occasionally, she will produce a smile.

Fifteen months ago, when I first met her, Freda could walk. She would incessantly pace the walls of the memory care unit. I learned, whenever I arrived, to sidle up to Freda and merge with her pacing. When I was in step with her, Freda would take hold of my hand. Once, as we were moving along in this way, I spoke the words of Psalm 23. When I was done, Freda stopped, lifted my hand, and kissed it.

Now when I visit, the room is usually dim. Freda is in bed, still and quiet. I check to see if she is breathing, hoping she is not. Yet, still, she is.

I sit quietly. I lift my hands over her. I whisper Scripture and prayers.

Here it is: I have learned to become still. I stare at Freda's face. I gaze upon her gaping mouth, her slack tongue, the tiny blue veins on her forehead, her bony face – her entire ruined form. After a while, an unbidden voice rises from my soul, and I hear it say, "So. This is You."

Yes, I say to God, "So, this is You, then." I dwell in that space. Anybody can stand on a stage and say commanding things about God and cause people to swoon. Any good vocalist can move your heart with music. The fickle Church crowd moves from venue to venue, looking for their latest vapid fix.

This, though – this space with Freda, this is my sanctuary. Suffering cannot pretend and does not lie.

This is where I see God.

My Church Math No Longer Adds Up

Jed is not, exactly, my hospice patient. Lana, his wife, is. When I first began chaplain visits with Lana,

Un Mediated

however, I began bringing donuts to Jed.

Jed cannot hear, see, or speak. He is, however, always knitting. A line of yarn stretches from his fingers, around his big toe, and back again to his knitting needles. Piles of Jed's fabric are stacked against the wall on the side of his bed. I do not know how Jed accomplishes this.

When I enter Lana and Jed's room, Lana is often sleeping, gulping oxygen from a tube in her nose. If she is awake, though, she sees the little white bag in my hand, and motions with her eyes toward Jed. She wants him to be happy.

I go to Jed and carefully touch his shoulder. He startles, turns his face toward me, and emits a loud sound, like "Hnuuhunh?" I reach in the bag and pull out the donut. I lift one of his hands and put the donut into it. Jed takes a moment to feel the texture. He puts the donut to his nose. Then he starts hollering. Jed sounds like a pod of seals.

While he is hooting, Jed reaches up his other hand, takes hold of mine, and kisses it. Sometimes I rub his brush-cutted head. He is hollering the whole time. Staff from the facility hear the ruckus, come to the door, peek in, then smile and call out, "It's OK – Jeddie just got his donut."

I get to see Jed for fifteen minutes every other week. It's about the holiest thing I do in my life right now.

It's not much, I know. The staff in that facility – they are the holy ones. Every day and night, they change

Simple **Faith**. Pure **Love**.

Jed's diapers and endure Lana's insults. It's only this: I've been to seminary. I have prayed, fasted, and memorized the Bible. I have heard sermons from the world's best preachers. I have sung worship songs in sanctuaries and stadiums. I have preached sermons that made people gush and cry. That felt good.

But with Jed, pure and simple, I feel like I am touching Jesus. Or Jesus is touching me. If only for a moment.

In my previous life, I operated with a complicated religious math equation in my mind:

> Pray + Church + Sermons + Worship Music + Theological Study + Bible Instruction + Christian Friends + Strenuous Moral Rectitude + Tithing
>
> **EQUALS...**
>
> A Christian life, A Happy life, A Successful and fruitful faith ... "I belong to God."

Yes, I was a sweat-soaked preacher of Religious Math:

> Preach about Jesus and Salvation + "Let's all pray and study the Bible" + lead the meetings + identify a vision + motivate believers + keep the organists from killing the guitarists + keep the big givers happy + visit the members in time of trouble + Try to convince the partiers to stop drinking + try to make the spouse abusers stop beating their spouses + try to keep everybody's penises and vaginas

channeling correctly + buy lots of coffee and, yes, *donuts* for the happy members + keep the nursery and youth group and Sunday school staffed with volunteers + **solve all our doctrinal disputes** + make a vision statement and mission statement + **issue statements about pressing moral issues** + keep people happy + **and then do even more to keep restless, religious people happy** + print bumper stickers to show other drivers how happy our members are at our church.

EQUALS...

A Happy, Unified Church, A Well-funded church, and a Salary, Success, and Happiness as a pastor-person.

And *then*: *If* we get all of that together. *If* we can get the whole group satisfied, *then* we are ready to do "outreach." We'll make a committee for that. I had this idea that, at the tail-end of all my mighty strivings, people would see our witness. "Look how friendly we are!" "Look at all the fun we have!" "Look at this happy place Jesus made!" People would get saved, or at least other already-saved people, unhappy elsewhere, will join *our* happy bunch. And the church will grow.

After that, **then**, we'll appoint a special group of specially committed, commissioned, and trained people to go and meet Jed.

Yay!

No, not "yay." It just wasn't adding up for me anymore. God stripped me down naked and dragged me through the eye of a needle. All I had left to do was visit people like Jed.

Jed, I suspect, would be the "side stuff" that Russell Moore's pastor-friend talked about. In my search to experience Jesus, I'm asking: Why not totally bypass a religion that thinks that way? In Jesus' mind, Jed was not the side stuff, but the *Main Stuff*.

What, then, if I put Jed first in line? For me, this is an unmediated experience with Christ. For most of my life, I have been busy, instead, with many things.

I feel the dissonance of this: I believe that being a pastor can be holy work. I have experienced the influence of God's Spirit in pastoral ministry. The churches I served blessed me immensely in every way. Beautiful people, who live as powerful examples of Jesus, attend churches and depend on those worship experiences to fuel their faith. My pastor-friends fulfill their callings, and I hold them in high esteem.

In my own journey, though, I came to a breaking point. In that moment, God took my sweaty face in both her hands and gently directed my gaze to something I was missing, or to something I needed.

Something unmediated by humanly manufactured religion.

The Cosmic Good Samaritan

Jesus' Parable of the Good Samaritan, I believe, is his story about himself. It is him, stooping down to lift and carry pretty-much-dead humanity. He said, "Go and do likewise" because that's how we will meet him.

Un Mediated

I figure the closer I can get to that, the better. If I can let that message take primacy in my heart and mind with regard with humanity in general, the better it will be for encountering him.

I would like to offer this: Take a careful measure of the output of your religious life. Where is the energy going? Take the parts of your religion, hold them in your palms, and examine them in the light. Is this a thing of which Jesus said, "Go and do likewise?"

If the answer is "No," I am trying to diminish or disregard that thing's role, or its thought process, in my life. Not that I have already attained this, but that's where I'm trying to go. For me, this has meant separating myself from the system and mindset of the Christianity I have known.

Theology Later

My friends laugh at the irony: In my new denomination, I am viewed, not unkindly, as a *conservative*. I still retain a few theological concepts from my past. I live a very buttoned-down life.

Yet, in the eyes of The Church, I am a liberal. For one thing, I believe God's love shines down upon, and lives within, people who don't live according to the theology and morals defined by the traditional Christian Church. I believe divine light and beauty resides in and flows through people who do not know or believe in Jesus. I have lately experienced God in this way of believing and living.

Simple **Faith**. Pure **Love**.

Suppose you don't believe like this. You think, because of my Universalist tendencies, I have wandered from the truth and betrayed the Gospel of Salvation and abandoned the finished work of Jesus from the cross and the requirements of faith. It's a big deal for you, maybe, to think of yourself as a chosen one and a saved one and that therefore you possess the finished truth. You think, maybe, that I am a false teacher.

Today, we both walk out the door into the world. Each of us, on our way, encounter someone who is suffering the miseries of life in this fallen world.

Is the wounded, miserable person "saved" or "damned?" Is this person one of "The Chosen?" If I help this person, is the person going to believe in Jesus? If the person's suffering is of their own making, and if I help them, am I "enabling" them? Is this person going to change their sinful behaviors?

Neither you nor I know the answer to any of those questions. Even if you believe in a line that separates your imaginings of "the saved" and "the damned," Jesus the Samaritan does not let us distinguish.

If theology is important to you, fine. I agree with you; it can be important and worthy work. I think, though, that Jesus is telling us to worry about it later. I have found spiritual peace by letting my moral and theological judgments go. *Until sometime later.*

Caveat: If we fill our lives serving suffering humanity, "later" always keeps turning into *more* "later."

Un Mediated

The Divine Synapse

One day, doing my rounds at the hospital, I entered the room of a retired banker. He consented to my visit, but said, with a friendly, but serious face, "You should know, Chaplain, that I am an atheist."

I assured him that it was no problem and proceeded to not talk about God. Ironically, as I was determined not to talk about God, the banker seemed determined to do so. He had good reasons for his atheism. Then he asked me why I believe in God. Spiritually lost as I was, I searched for a rock-bottom truth within me. What I found in the desert sand of my heart was this:

"Honestly, I am not sure of my own faith right now. I have lost much of what I formerly believed. There is only thing for me now: I walk around this hospital, and meet all kinds of suffering people, from all sorts of backgrounds. I find that when I get next to a person, that when two human beings are heart to heart, that's where I find God. Like, I experience God right now, just with you and me, right here. That's all I got."

He nodded his head and was quiet for a moment. Then we talked about other things – his illness, his family, his former work-life. Eventually I stood to leave. I did not offer to say a prayer, and did not throw in a quick, "God bless you."

Just as I made it to the door, he said, "Hey, Chaplain, just so you know, about ten minutes ago, I started believing in God again."

I did not feel, in that moment, any sense of "Whew!

Simple **Faith**. Pure **Love**.

Someone got saved!" I am not telling you about him now to promote a strategy for getting people through the goalposts of heaven.

It's only this: Even if he had never said that last line, I still would have felt that I had stood on holy ground.

I think of it as a *Divine Synapse*. Human beings, heart to heart, together, suspended in divine energy. Not bound by doctrinal agreement or manufactured religion or skin color or national identity or life choices. Just compassion. Whenever I am suspended in that space, I feel divine peace. It is a fully human experience, yet I feel the unmediated presence of God. Yep: The Unmediated Synapse. That's all I have, pure and simple. There I am, there we are, floating in the hand of God.

Jayne's Kiss

Lorilee is a 72-year-old breathing skeleton. Jayne, one of my co-workers at our hospice company, is the skeleton's nurse.

One day, I was sitting by Lorilee's bed, politely offering prayers from about two feet away.

Jayne happened to show up while I was there. She walked in, greeted me, set down her bag, and came to Lorilee. Jayne took Lorilee's hand and rubbed it. I could see that Jayne was turning Lorilee's hand as she held it, surveying Lorilee's arm for bruises and scratches. Jayne murmured and fussed over Lorilee. Jayne stroked Lorilee's head. Lorilee smiled, then, and I watched in slow-motion as Jayne leaned over and put her face, her cheek, right there against Lorilee's cheek, close to her lips, and kissed her.

Jayne, in that moment, to me, looked like Jesus. Jayne gets right in there with the dried mucus and saliva.

As I know all too well, there is a way to care from a church sanctuary, from an abstract distance. I have stood on platforms and spoke passionately about loving people, but they were imaginary people, and it was fantasy love. I was thinking that by being rigorously moral, or by working hard at being nice, I was being a "witness."

The Compassion of Jesus is from another universe. It's what Jayne does. It gets into the grist and guts of human suffering.

Jesus In Weakness

Sometimes a rock star or a mega-athlete announces they have converted to Christianity. I remember being so happy at times like that. It made Christianity cool. These converts were beautiful, or handsome, or sculpted, or skilled. These are the people we invited to speak at youth conferences and megachurches. They made great sermon material.

I used to like a strong God, too. I believed in and needed a divinity who thunders from a mountain, and who controls everything. In the same way, The Church, these days, in its vanity, conjures for itself images of Jesus as a warrior, strapped with belts of bullets, smiting people with the breath of his mouth.

Now, I find Jesus in Dawn, who is 84 years old, and has just enough of her mental capacity left to know she is losing her mental capacity. She holds my hand and speaks of her fear. She wants to die. Dawn also has a gastrointestinal problem. While she pours out to me her search for God and her wish to die, she is emitting high, tight little burps. Then, while I was praying with her, out came this loud, deep belch. All the way through the prayer Dawn kept saying, "Sorry . . . oh, excuse me . . . oh. . . . "

Nobody will invite Dawn to speak at a conference. I don't need the celebrities anymore.

I find Jesus with Dawn. I find Jesus in weakness.

Sacrament From A Tin Can

If I visit someone, and if I happen to show up during lunch, the overwhelmed staff is quite happy to let me assist.

I drape what used to be called a bib, but now, for dignity's sake, is called a "clothing protector," over the front of the person. I sit next to them, fork or spoon in hand, and lift food to their mouths.

I hold the green beans, which have just recently been poured out from a tin can, in front of them. I can feel the air from their nostrils as I hold the fork to their lips.

They open their mouths like birds. I say the person's name, and as I place the food on their tongues I whisper, "The Body of Christ for you."

Un Mediated

These days, this is how I administer the sacrament.

Anybody can do this, simple and pure. You don't have to wait for an ordained person or a prescribed liturgy to feed and nourish others unto eternal life.

Locked Dementia Unit

Every facility has a special dementia unit. You would hardly notice, because this unit is separated from the rest of us by discreetly painted double doors. I go the door, press the doorbell, and wait. Eventually, from the other side of the door, I hear the beeping sounds of the code. A staff person opens the locked door and lets me in. I enter a menagerie of human dysfunction.

Frank lurches past, pushing his walker. One of his feet doesn't quite work, and he drags it along.

Jessica paces the walls, muttering, all day long. Later, I am wheeling a patient named Cindy to her room so we can have a private prayer. When we get to Cindy's room, we find that Jessica has finally stopped pacing; she has wandered into Cindy's room and is contentedly emptying her bowels into Cindy's toilet.

Linda is walking around, too, tidying magazines, making sure all the chairs are pushed in at their tables, and trying to adjust pictures frames, even though they are bolted to the wall. Linda tidies things - all day long. She confronts her fellow residents, trying to tidy them up too. She fusses with their clothing, and they get mad, and sometimes push her away. Every facility I visit, it seems, has a Linda, a fussbudget who bustles around tidying everything until people get pissed. Or, there is a Douglas, who marches around trying to fix non-existent problems with light switches and furniture. Douglas always gives out rambling instructions, and people get pissed.

One man sits in a chair, grinding his teeth. It sounds like a large metal comb being raked across the edge of sheet metal. All day long. There is a woman who grinds her teeth, too. She sounds like a very loud cricket. All day long.

Janice, over the year I have visited her, has been immobile. She has been able to do nothing, it has seemed, but sit in her wheelchair. If Janice is going to get from her wheelchair into her bed, staff people must help her. I sit next to Janice's wheelchair and hold her limp hand to pray. One of our nurses, though, recently found Janice in a male resident's room, *standing* next to his bed, her hand firmly gripping his erect penis. Janice had left her wheelchair in the hall. When Janice is motivated, she can really move.

One guy, at lunch, is clinking his spoon on the edge of his soup bowl, like people do with their wine glasses at a wedding when they want the couple to kiss. This man never stops with the bowl dinging. His face is hanging over his bowl, his mouth is drooling into it, and he is staring absently at the far wall, tap-tap-tapping that spoon, all through lunch. People get mad and tell him to shut up, but he does not, and cannot, stop.

Three silver-haired women are at a lunch table. I am two tables over, entering records into my computer tablet, when one of these ladies erupts with,

UnMediated

"Shut up, you bitches!"

Stephanie, when I enter the locked unit, always hurries to me: "Sir! Sir? Can you help me?" She needs a ride to Kalamazoo, or she wants to find a recipe for butterscotch cookies, or she is trying to find a coffee shop. When I admit to her that I cannot fix this for her, she purses her lips in frustration, and pushes her walker away.

When my co-workers, the home health aides, enter these locked dementia units, they exit with scratches and bruises on their arms. Elderly women pull the aides' hair; elderly men slap and pinch.

It used to be that, when I was done with my visits and was ready to leave, when the staff person would come and enter the code for me again and would open the door to let me out of the unit, I would gasp after the fresh air and feel released again into the normal world. Not anymore.

I have come to the point where the "outside world" looks and feels like just one large, locked dementia unit.

I think of Jesus, walking the streets, everyone lurching along, coming up to him and babbling about their delusional desires and demanding his help, everybody punching, grabbing, scratching, groping, and cussing their way down the road. All day long.

Religious people who sit in church are no different. A church, too, is its own locked dementia unit.

And there's me, pacing around, fussing over everyone and everything, incessantly trying to tidy everything up for God.

We are all the same. Our planet is a locked dementia unit.

Amazingly, Jesus coded in.

It Cannot Be Wrong to Seek a New Way

Jesus looks straight at us and tells us what kind life he wants us to create.

Then we go out and build systems precisely contrary to his description. We construct religious pleasure-centers. We use his name to anoint our moral power and condone our racism and violence. We ask him to bless our systems of financial and political control.

Then we sing and pray and tell him we did it all for him. This a fantasy of our own creation.

It is the stuff of a dementia unit.

It cannot be wrong for you to seek spiritual peace and sanity apart from those systems.

Why I Keep Saying "Sometimes"

I may have left you the impression that I am holier than I am.

Just to be clear: Often, I *don't* encounter Jesus in my visits with people. There are times when my heart is cold. Usually, on a Friday afternoon, I just want to get this visit over with and go home. On occasion, I dislike a patient with whom I am visiting. In some visits,

UnMediated

people's fluids and body functions just plain gross me out. There are visits in which I do not represent Jesus well at all, and in which I do not encounter him. There are days when I wonder if I imagine this whole "Jesus" thing.

Sometimes, though, I encounter Jesus. Yes, I do believe so.

"Sometimes" is saving my soul.

UnMediated

Simple **Faith**. Pure **Love**.

Un Mediated

Simple **Faith**. Pure **Love**.

SECTION SEVEN

Dumpster Theology

Thoughts On God & Faith

UnMediated

Earlier I told you about crawling into a cannon and lighting my own fuse. I said that I was "sailing and flailing" and haven't landed yet, and yet I was spiritually free.

I had come to a crisis. My spirit was shattered. My soul just wasn't buying what The Church was selling. I believed in God with my head, but not my heart. Eventually I started asking myself, "Well, what *is* my heart telling me about God?"

My heart still is fed and nourished by the faith of my past. I still believe in Jesus; I am a sinner saved by grace. I believe in baptism, and the Lord's Supper. Some of the creeds and confessions of my past are core documents of the UCC. I could show you a list of many checked boxes.

The list, however, doesn't work anymore for me. I want a mural of divine color and light. I yearn for unmediated things.

David James Duncan, in his novel *Sun House*, creates a character named Jervis. Having left the Catholic Church, and after a series of mystic experiences, Jervis caught a vision of a "gigantic old dumpster out behind Mother Church."[13] Jervis picks up the shreds of God he believes were discarded by The Church and builds his own incarnational theology, which he calls "Dumpster Catholicism." What follows are the beginnings of my own dumpster diving.

13- See David James Duncan, *Sun House* (Little, Brown 2023), 149.

Simple **Faith**. Pure **Love**.

These concepts don't answer everything for me, and they might not answer anything at all for you. I only mention them here in case it helps you find some peace and freedom. At the very least, maybe you will feel encouraged to identify some core faith concepts in your own soul.

Jesus Alone

Think of Christianity as a big vat of Jell-O.

When I was growing up, my grandmothers loaded their Jell-O with other stuff: Canned fruit, or worse, shredded carrots (it was like eating a slimy hairball).

Religion is packed with stuff, too. There, stuck in the goo, is the American Flag. Also, there is money, representing capitalism and earth's treasure. At the bottom is a building, the institution of The Church.

Behold. This is the jiggling mass called "Christianity."

This shining vat of Jell-O stew is not the divine, unmediated love about which Jesus taught.

Jesus is flesh dwelling among us, walking in the world, extracting people from the grip of mere earthly religion and into a different way of thinking and being—into a pure, simple, free way of being known and being loved.

People ask me if I still believe in Jesus. Yes, only without the Jell-O, and without all the imbedded, merely earthly stuff.

Un Mediated

Jesus First (Not Moses, Paul, or Preachers)

Much of what is called Christianity, as I have experienced it and taught it, is a tower of Mosaic Law and violent Old Testament stories with Jesus, like a cheerleader, perched at the top. Or, it is a mechanical thought system, humming with the legal and logical precision of Pauline theology, with Jesus' blood lubricating the machinery. Or, it is a social concoction arising from the fevered imaginations of preachers. Or, it is a tool of the systems of government and finance.

Jesus is Other.

He refused to attach his life to Empire's political or financial flow. He chose to possess nothing. He did not teach a clear moral code, other than compassion and love. He eschewed adulation, did not muster a base of support for his own glory, never once built a building. He did not audition disciples for their singing abilities. He never put on a show or whipped people into a state of emotional ecstasy.

He lived in the world. He told of God's unfailing love for us. He taught, and lived, mercy and compassion.

I have made a decision: Moses bows to Jesus. So does Paul. If either Moses or Paul taught anything that is different in tone and style from what Jesus said, then I must either adjust or discard what they said. If a preacher promotes a view of humanity that is different than that of Jesus, I ignore the preacher.

Simple **Faith**. Pure **Love**.

To what degree I can find Jesus, he must be second to no one. There are myriad interpreters of the message of Jesus (scholars, preachers, and church pew pundits). Even the scribes who constructed the Bible scribbled their views into the manuscripts.

I am interpreting Jesus, too. I am putting him, first and foremost, in his simplest form, at the center of my heart, hoping to imbibe and faintly replicate how he thought about and interacted with humanity. I don't need anyone to tell me more. I don't need to go into a physical structure. I don't need special lighting. I don't need a secret spiritual formula. I don't need mediated teachings, twisted by human hands.

Jesus said: Go into your room. Close the door. Talk to God. Open the door, enter the world, and serve humanity with compassions of Christ.

At the core, for me, that's it.

For now, until my nerve endings grow back and develop new pathways of sensation (if they ever do), I have found spiritual peace in throwing out any religion which places Moses, Paul, or anyone into a place of primacy. I have abandoned the tortured process of syncretizing their teachings into a thought-system with Jesus.

Jesus' teaching, all by itself, is quite enough to handle on his own. Every day, for me, is another stumbling attempt.

I am suggesting a relentless focus on the person, life, example, and teaching of Jesus. If you have time and energy and inclination for a church service after that, go for it.

Abandon The Abraham Project

People told John the Baptist they were children of Abraham. John responded by saying that God can make children of Abraham from stones.

Any Divine Being who can create body parts, sperm, and egg can create another physical descendent of a religion. Additionally, anybody can become proficient as a child of religion by *trying really hard*, in the same way that people, by trying hard, accomplish great feats. I saw a contestant on a talent show who placed a metal cylinder on a table, then piled a sequence of chairs twenty feet high on top of the cylinder, and then, on top of that stack, did a handstand. How many years of intense personal training did it take to accomplish that? What if someone devoted ten percent of that kind of focus and effort on becoming morally pure and theologically accurate for God?

Jesus did not institute a training program for highly motivated and well-behaved people. When he said, "make disciples," I don't think he had in mind to indoctrinate successful children of religion. Anybody can gather a pile of stones.

I am seeking to know and experience Jesus. In my lost condition, I am giving up on the Abraham project and distancing myself from its devotees and enforcers.

Simple **Faith**. Pure **Love**.

For now, I find relief in meeting with people who can't accomplish anything and are at the end of all their strivings. Maybe someday there will be something more. For now, this is where I find peace.

Unity, Wayne's Way

Jesus prayed that we all might be one. It's not working. We currently have 45,000 Christian denominations in the world, each one claiming exclusive Truth. Doctrine, theology, and a worship industry do not create unity.

I like how Wayne does it. One day, I worked alongside him. Wayne is a chaplain from another hospice company. Wayne walked into the common room and found his patient seated at a table with seven other women. They were playing Bingo. Wayne pulled a chair into the circle and sat next to his patient. He helped both his patient, who was on his right, and another resident, who was on his left, place their plastic chips on the right squares, because their minds couldn't quite keep track of the numbers, and because their hands were shaky and their vision was cloudy. He laughed and told a few jokes. When the Bingo game was done, Wayne stayed in the circle, and sang "You Are My Sunshine." Some of the women, with smiling eyes and nodding heads, sang along.

What Wayne did, and the essence of how Wayne was, match my imagination of how Jesus created unity. For example, when Jesus went to Matthew's house for a party – maybe that's how Jesus' brand of unity

Un Mediated

was. Jesus did this at Zacchaeus' house party, too. Jesus was *with* people, and seemed to like them, as they were, raw and unfiltered. Matthew and Zacchaeus, and their house guests, sinners all, perceived Jesus as a friend. Yep: That's what they called him: "Friend of sinners." I think this is how Jesus created unity with humanity.

There is different imagination of "unity." In this vision, you gather, say, four hundred people in a room. Before people enter the worship space, you decide what the doctrines and the rules are. Before the gathering, you make clear who is welcome into this space and who isn't. Within this bandwidth, the preacher produces a master craft of language and emotion which hits all the marks, and everyone is juiced. The crowd stands to sing, "Blest Be the Tie That Binds," and many shed tears. Four hundred people, out of a planet full of humanity, having encased themselves in this prefabricated bubble, feeling that they have attained what Jesus taught about unity, all the while mentally and emotionally cutting off people who believe differently. So you have a bubble of four hundred people here, another bubble of four thousand people over there, and big denominational bubbles, too.

I think Jesus had Wayne's kind of unity in mindJesus was envisioning that we would initiate and instigate a simple, spiritual, open, compassionate friendship with other human beings around us, just as they are, in all their diversity. That we would carry an aroma of humility, curiosity, and safety about us. This would be the spirit of Jesus, uniting humanity. Think of it: The Church, Friend of the World, and Unifier of Humanity.

Bobblehead Jesus

For a sermon, I sewed a bobblehead Jesus onto the shoulder of my suitcoat. During the sermon, I asked questions about moral issues. For the answers, I looked at the bobblehead doll and shrugged my shoulder. Sure enough, no matter what I wanted, each time Jesus said "yes."

I think of all the behavioral decisions church members have pondered.

Is it OK to hunt deer on Sunday instead of going to church? For guys who had already decided that it was permissible, Jesus bobbled "yes."

Can I have sex before I am married or not? In this, Jesus gets bounced and bobbled a lot.

Think of us: Mormons, Seventh-day Adventists, Baptists. "Here is the way of living that pleases God." We all think we know.

I understand that. I have beliefs about "good living" for God, too. Mostly, though, I think we bobble our way along.

In this light, I look at the stories of Jesus' ministry. Look at all the people who tried to bobble him!

>Can I divorce someone?
>
>Do I pay taxes to Caesar or not?
>
>Make my brother give my share

Un Mediated

of the inheritance!

Sabbath this, Sabbath that.

Are you going to make Israel great again?

He eluded and confounded them all.

There were other people who sought out Jesus, however, who had no energy left for bobblehead games. These people were miserable, exhausted, and scared. They threw themselves down. They called out for divine help.

I bobble Jesus all the time. I shrug and dance through life, imagining he approves my moves.

I can't bobble divine compassion, though. It's always putrid smelling, wrinkled, or oozing. It requires sacrifice. It's the thing I would rather not do. To this, Jesus always says "yes." That's where the divine action is.

I Reject Christian-based Violence and Aggression

If there is one area in which Christianity has bobbled Jesus, it would be in the roiling mix of nation, power, and aggression. In Jesus' day, the crowd invested him with their dreams to reclaim the glory of Israel. He repeatedly avoided and rejected their nationalist hopes. Jesus refused to raise either a human army or an angelic one to accomplish his mission.

The Bible shows us Jesus, raised from the dead. Just before he is lifted to heaven in the ascension story, the disciples ask him their one last burning question: "Lord, are you at this time going to restore the Kingdom to Israel?" In essence: "Are you going to make Israel great again?" In the context of all they had witnessed of Jesus and the content of his life, think of the stupidity of that question.

Admittedly, Jesus' refusal is lame. Instead of correcting them firmly, he only re-directs them. It is an important re-direction, though: Make spiritual disciples, not religious soldiers. Obey his commands of love, non-violence, and forgiveness. Suffer violence, do not cause it. Don't overpower anyone in his name.

Jesus is not the armor-clad messiah of any one nation, including the United States of America. He is not the lapdog-bobblehead for anyone's internal aggression.

In the Old Testament, the Israelites bobbleheaded God by carrying the Ark of the Covenant into battle. It didn't work to do that with God then, and it will never work to carry Jesus like a totem into anyone's battles now.

On January 6, 2021, Religious Trumpists carried their totems into their battle on Washington D.C. They carried that picture of Jesus, on a stick, wearing a MAGA hat. They carried crosses. They carried posters bearing Jesus' name.

Reject any church that baptizes people with water from this toxic, idolatrous well. Avoid any church that will not openly confront this twisting of the message of Jesus.

It frightens me to say these things. Jesus said the

time will come when brother hands brother over to death. Religious violence will come to believers who live by peace. I am preparing for this to happen to me. It might also happen to you.

I don't know if I have the courage to live and die this way. I only know I cannot stay with a "Christianity" which either promotes or appeases White Nationalism and Religious Trumpism. I refuse to identify with a religion originating from Old Testament myths about Israel, and which proclaims from its bumper stickers "God, Guns, and Trump."

I Reject the Gospel of the Four Guys

The four richest guys in a church cornered the pastor. At the time, there was a discussion in The Church about LGBTQ+ persons, and my denomination had issued a hardline statement. The pastor was having doubts that the statement reflected what Jesus was all about and had expressed those doubts to a few people. The four rich guys said to him, "If you don't fully back that statement, or if you say anything contrary to it, we will withhold our offerings and pressure the other leaders of this church to fire you."

Now let's imagine you're in trouble and in spiritual need. You want to find God and "get your spiritual life back on track." Know this: If you walk through the doors of that church, what you will hear is something that sounds good and has the appearance of godliness but is The Gospel According to The Four Guys (and I'm not talking about Matthew, Mark, Luke, or John). You will be entering a sphere of theology and practice in which Jesus has been lassoed, tranquilized, caged, harnessed, and put to slave labor by human power-players. Jesus did not have in mind for you to submit your soul to those rich guys' man-made religion.

Think, now: Mega churches. Denominations. Christian colleges and religious organizations. All driven and dictated by the donors' bandwidth. All those "leaders" dropping to the ground, rolling in the Four Guys' dirty money.

In all of this, we have abandoned the realm of basic teaching from the Bible that "the worker is worthy of their hire," which is about churches generously caring for their pastor's financial needs. We have left the realm of good pastors who compromise and who listen to the wise voices of their congregants. We have left the realm in which people use their money as cheerful givers.

Instead, with the Four Guys, we have entered the realm of rich and powerful people mangling the Gospel. They jam their fists into the field of God's pure love and ruin it. God did not intend for your soul to languish in the wreckage of that collapse.

You benefit more from the unmediated Gospel of the simple and the small. From a Gospel which has been conceived in the synapse of human-to-human, divine compassion. In your spiritual distress, through the blur of your tears, you might not see this clearly.

Peter said to a man named Simon, "May your money perish with you, because you thought you could buy the gift of God with money." Peter might as well be speaking to the Four Rich Guys.

What Is "The Gospel?"

I keep throwing that word around. What is *The Gospel?*

In The Church's sphere, the pat answer is faith in Jesus. It's heaven or hell. This involves an Old Testament religion of conditional love, obedience, judgment, groveling, and punishment. If that's what Jesus came to say, he was a failure in that regard. He did not stand on street corners preaching, "Turn or burn." It was not his message.

I must admit, I resonate with this sphere, because the Gospel, for me, includes Atonement. I have sin in me. I am a fallen person. Nevertheless, out of sheer grace, without my deserving it all, God reckons me as an object of divine love. I accept this with a believing heart.

From within that same sphere, it is tempting for me to advocate a Gospel of clean living, hard work, and success.

Jesus' sphere of the Gospel, though, is wider, longer, higher, and deeper than all of that. The Gospel is not just about me, getting saved. I believe Jesus' Gospel applies to everyone and is unlimited. In our fallen condition, his Gospel for humanity is: "Protect shamed people from stoning." His Gospel is God, gathering the crippled and the lame from "the highways and the by-ways" for the feast of heaven. His

Simple **Faith**. Pure **Love**.

Gospel is acceptance for lepers. His Gospel is: Be a friend of "sinners." His Gospel is Divine Compassion for all of us, stuck here in hell's misery.

In these days, I think The Church has obsessed on the former sphere of the Gospel and has willfully neglected the latter.

Don't settle for a small Gospel. You, settling, would be like the kid in Jesus' story of the Prodigal Son. The kid had wasted everything his father had given him and finally was ruined and starving. At first, the kid was on the verge of settling for pig food, but then settled on the plan to go home and grovel. What he found instead was extravagant, un-failing divine love.

Why settle for a man-made, limited, small Gospel, rather than what Jesus told us about?

Unconditional Love

As I do my hospice work, I often drive past a billboard which says, "Genuine Christians Obey Jesus."

First, a question: Does the "obey" refer to selling your possessions, refusing to build bigger barns for gaining wealth, welcoming the poor and the weak, rejecting weapons and violence, and stooping down to give compassion to the world?

Or is the "obey" referring to not aborting babies, not being gay, and to being a patriotic American?

Beyond that, the real issue of the billboard's message is the invisible sword of "IF" hanging above it. What is a "*genuine* Christian?"

Un Mediated

"Believe in the Lord Jesus and you shall be saved." This is what I have been taught, and what I have preached. "You get to go to heaven if you believe. And if you obey."

I have concluded that the Gospel of Conditional Love does not work. It does not produce the divine peace Jesus talked about. "If" is not how Jesus lived, or what he taught.

Many of the elderly dying people I meet have lived the billboard's message. They have obeyed, not perfectly, but strenuously. They have tried so very hard. They have been "genuine Christians."

Yet, when I enter their faith world and dwell with them there, when I take on their divine concepts and their religious language, when I gently wonder with them about their sense of peace as death comes near, they are often genuinely afraid.

They are not just afraid of dying. They are afraid because they are unsure if they are good enough to make it to heaven. When I read for them from the Bible about eternal life, they say, "Well, I *hope* so." This is more than being unsure about the mystery of eternal life. When they say, "I hope so," they mean they are not sure they qualify. Think of it: All those sermons. All those prayers. All those tithes. All the volunteer shifts in the nursery, or those years on the church board. At the end of it, no peace.

When I was teenager, one of our teachers took us on a tour of a soda pop factory. Pop cans, in the final step of their journey to packaging, came whizzing past, single file, on a one-lane conveyor belt. Every 45 seconds or so, I heard a "Ka-chunk" sound, and then saw a pop can flying, spinning through the air on a downward arc and landing in a heap of other cans. I asked what that was about. The tour guide said that a tiny scale had been imbedded into the conveyor belt, and with it a pneumatic punch. Any underweight cans were catapulted into the discard pile.

Over my entire life, I have lived with that feeling of being underweight, fearing God's pneumatic punch. Over my career, I preached with that "Ka-chunk" sound in my mind. Embedded in the term "Genuine Christian" is God's fist, ready to punch. With God, it is never enough.

I am aware that the Bible, in many places, teaches conditional love. Even Jesus appears to talk that way sometimes. Well, just as The Church chooses to ignore Jesus' teaching when it comes to the abandonment of wealth, the rejection of empire, and the eschewing of violence as a means of accomplishing his mission, I choose to ignore the places where Jesus *seems* to teach conditional love.

I believe God has unhooked the wires to the scale and dismantled the pneumatic punch. Jesus came to show us and tell us this message.

Simple Joy

Fear, I've always thought, is good. My childhood preacher's favorite "Call to Worship" at the beginning of the worship service was, "Surely, it is a dreadful thing to fall into the hands of the Living God."

Divine Dread, so I've thought, has kept me from sinning and from wrecking my life; it led me to Jesus and saved me from a destiny in hell. That kind of fear, however, has also crippled my faith and choked my soul. My spiritual life has been one of quaking, trembling, and groveling.

Lynnette shows me a better way. Even though, in her dementia, she cannot find her own room without help, and even though Lynette's diapers must be changed for her, nevertheless her face is always smiling. Lynette has the gift of joy. Her joy is natural and has grown like a lily in a field under the perpetually loving gaze of her earthly father.

Lynette tells me often, as if each time is the first time, about her dad. Whenever she does, her face is beaming, and she says, "Ooooh – he was a good man."

From the fragments of the stories Lynette tells, it seems that she was in trouble a lot. Her stories of her father take place in a principal's office, or in a grocery store where she attempted shoplifting, or in some situation where someone is mad at her. One story involves an angry preacher, offended by Lynette's behavior in church.

Lynette's father, in every story, stands by her side, listening carefully to what the aggrieved person has to say. He agrees that he will pay back what she stole or replace what she broke. He turns to her, and she knows it is time for her to apologize.

Simple **Faith**. Pure **Love**.

This is how every one of Lynette's stories ends: At the end of it all, when they are alone, her father puts his hand on her shoulder, smiles, and says, "Now, Lynette, you're not going to do that again, are you?"

She says, "No, Daddy, I won't." (Even though it seems she often did.)

Her father hugs her. Every time.

Lynette has pure and simple joy because, even in her addled mind, she thinks of God that way.

Lynette was a bit of a wild child, I think. As she grew up, though, she was a happy child. Now, in dementia, she continues to be happy. This, among the folks I visit, is rare.

I wish I had Lynette's joy. I am seeking it by thinking and believing differently about God.

Hell and Heaven, Here And Now

More than ever, I believe in eternal life. It was at the heart of Jesus' message.

Jesus, though, didn't spend as much time as we do talking about heaven, defining who gets to go there, and who doesn't. He didn't set up a stage, like a chalk artist, in all the towns and villages, creating neon visions of Heaven. He never avoiding the hard questions by blowing fantasy bubbles. He didn't obsess about the Chosen Ones rewarded with clouds, harps, or the Great Gated Community in the Sky.

He focused on our miserable condition, here and now. He gave up all other glories and entered human suffering. He taught us to get down in it and show compassion there, too.

I suspect that most of my religion has been, and still is, a socio-economic escape from, human misery. Religion becomes an illusion, and a justification for "the good life." This can work quite well, until you come to the point when you must have a tube shoved up you so that your bladder can empty into a bag, and/or until another tube gets placed into your nostrils to deliver oxygen. There is no escape: Beautiful people, lovely lives, and tubes.

Jesus didn't fix that and gave no illusions about that.

Hell is what we're living now. Heaven is not a sermon or a song.

It is compassion, here and now, in our miseries.

Still a Mess

I don't believe in sermons, but sometimes I preach them. I don't have any faith in corporate worship, but most Sundays I get together with people, sing songs, and listen to a talk. I don't believe in human ideas about God, but I just wrote a little book with ideas about God.

I am still lost, still a bit numb, still a bit of a mess. I don't have it all figured out.

That's better for me. If any preacher or religious leader projects an attitude of "I have come down from the mountain, and I know the will of God for you," I reject their message instantly. I am repulsed by anything that makes Jesus into a consumerist

Simple **Faith**. Pure **Love**.

show. There is no space in me, either, for breathy, religious fantasy.

I want Jesus, pure, simple, and unadorned. If something I have said here helps you, I am thankful. If not, ignore it, because I might be wrong.

UnMediated

Simple **Faith**. Pure **Love**.

SECTION EIGHT
What if I am Wrong?

Un Mediated

The Tragedy We Already Know

Yes, I do worry about being wrong. What if everybody leaves church? What if everybody just does what is right in their own eyes? What happens to America? Do we all just become morally boneless chickens, with no strength or structure for living? What if The Church does not raise up children? I wonder and worry.

I worry more, however, about the kind of world The Church has already produced, about what kind of world this would be if The Church ruled it as a theocracy, and what kind of children it is raising up now.

True story, for example: There is a neighborhood of Church friends living a very nice life right here in Ottawa County. They live in palatial homes. They gather as families on weekends. The kids play. The parents grill steaks and sample microbrews. The parents often talk about their church-lives, because they are all youth leaders, Sunday School teachers, and deacons. Also, a gay person lives in that neighborhood, and The Church families say crude and condemning things as they drive past. Also, the neighborhood church guys text each other pictures of naked women during the week. I wonder what kind of children *that* religion produces?

Another true story: A pastor-friend told me of his experience in a Zoom call with a group of local pastors, leaders in the conservative movement of my former denomination. The topic of this meeting was abortion. My friend left the call shaken. He told me,

"They were cold, and cruel. If my daughter was pregnant and scared, those pastors are *the last people in the world* I would want her to talk to." What kind of "culture of life" do those pastors (each of whom has their own set of "Four Guys") create?

When I was a pastor, during Covid, Alicia and I went for dinner at a restaurant which had adapted by creating outdoor seating. Our server was a girl from our church's youth group. She told us about the church people who had sometimes made her cry, because they came arguing, yelling, and making accusations against her and her other servers because of Covid safety protocols.

You think, maybe, that I am cherry-picking, and that it's not fair of me to highlight such horrible stories.

I believe, however, the beliefs and attitudes represented in these stories are deeply woven, like stained fabric, like a spiritual and mental illness, into the culture of The Church.

Think of a massive group of people, claiming to know what divine love is, yet exerting their power like cruel bullies in the world. Consider: What if you are seeking God and stumble into a group of religious people who have had their minds stoked with stories of sinners being speared to death and of a physical nation of Israel rising again to rule the world? But the greeters are friendly. The blueberry donuts, also, are quite fine.

Un Mediated

A good, kind and gentle-hearted Christian might say to me, "*I am not like that. My* church is not like that."

Wonderful. **Say it then**. Stop appeasing it. Confront the horror of the anti-Gospel. Articulate and proclaim a full Gospel of Love. But you can't, and your church won't, because of the Four Guys and all their Church friends.

Yes, I worry. I might be wrong. There's no way to know what kind of future a theology and practice of Unmediated Love would create. What we do know is what kind of world The Church has already created. We are left wondering what might have been.

What might the world have been if The Church had not used the Israelite stories to create a system of slavery? What kind of world would it have created if The Church had not used the Bible, the name of God, and a hell-baked idea of "Manifest Destiny" to perpetrate genocide against Indigenous peoples? We will never know.

As we have seen consistently in history, and as we see today, The Church will align itself with Empire and its systems. It will just keep on adding more layers of man-made, mangled, dangerous religion. I worry more about that.

What if people, stuck here in the misery of this locked dementia unit, turn to us, and do not find the heart of Christ? What if we who claim Jesus possess none of his divine compassion? If we, of all humans, have given our lives, our passions, our sermons, our tithes, and our songs unto just another earthly project of power and violence, we are most to be pitied.

You, however, have another option. A chance to write a new story with your life.

Writing a New Story

Earlier I mentioned to you my confession that I had wasted my life. The question still troubles me.

The Midnight Library, a novel by Matt Haig, has helped me. Haig imagines a place where all a person's potential lives are stored, like books on a shelf. For example, you date someone, and then choose to break it off. That choice closes the book of your life to that point and all the possibilities of what might have been. That book goes on the shelf. You meet someone else and marry. Another book. Kids? Another book.

In my case, choosing to be a pastor created a book. Turning down a job offer from a church – that choice creates a book. Then I accepted the job offer from another church. That becomes another life-book.

I am learning to bow my head and thank God for acceptance and grace through all the pages of my life – what I used to think, believe, and preach. It doesn't help me to wallow in guilt over it. The title of every chapter is love. Those old books – yes, they are mine, alright.

Now, at this writing, I am sixty-three years old. I only pray to write a new story. I want to live with a different heart, and a different approach to all things divine and human. Every page of this book, too, will

UnMediated

be flawed. I am trusting divine grace, light, and peace, upon every paragraph, every syllable.

Think of it: Today, and every day, God offers you the holy privilege of writing a new story.

Go ahead and laugh: My new story involves a church. I should explain that.

UnMediated

Simple **Faith**. Pure **Love**.

UnMediated

Simple Faith. Pure Love.

SECTION NINE
Safety & Spiritual Freedom

Un Mediated

Explaining How I Landed in a Church

I still don't believe in or trust corporate worship and don't listen to or sing Christian music. Yet, I am an ordained pastor, and most Sundays at 10:00 a.m. I am sitting in a church. If I explain it to you, maybe I will understand it better myself.

Remember the backdrop: Remember how the pastor from my former denomination reposted Rev. Joseph Rigney's blog? Rigney wrote admiringly of Old Testament priests doing violence to advance God's will. This, apparently, is Rigney's vision for Christianity. This is the vision which drives much of The Church today.

The pastor who reposted that, and his ordained kin, had hijacked the steering wheel of my former denomination. From their "Israelite Zealot" view of the Bible and Christianity, they had produced a document for the denomination which made clear that no person in a same-sex marriage and no trans person should hope in acceptance from a church. They also misapplied the historic confessions of the denomination. In the same way you would wrench the blades from a farm plow and weld them into a razor wire fence, they bent and refashioned the confessions to lock out LGBTQ persons and anyone supportive of them.

The denominational zealots, it seemed, could not sing their songs, offer up their prayers, or listen to their sermons on a Sunday morning without being rankled by the awareness that there might be a denominational church somewhere on that same Sunday in which a gay or trans person might be singing and praying too.

Not to mention the hormones of Religious Trumpism coursing through the veins of The Church.

All of which meant I would never fit in my former denomination again. I had trained to work as a chaplain, and, practically, I needed to be ordained in a denomination to do so. I was nervous about this. If there was a denominational "fit" for us, Alicia and I did not know where that might be. We were not attending any church and had no practical plan for doing so.

Alicia was Facebook friends, though, with a woman who was a pastor's wife. The pastor, from the United Church of Christ, was running as a Democrat for congress, of all places, here in the "Trump country" of Ottawa County, Michigan. This pastor, I thought, had ridiculous courage.

Trump followers were harassing him. Already they had been driving by the pastor's house and screaming vulgarities at the pastor's wife and children. Already they had been coming to the pastor's home in the night, spreading trash and beer cans on his front yard. Already they had smashed his mailbox.

Now, these Trump-inspired people had threatened physical violence, broadly, for a specific Sunday morning, against UCC churches. The pastor's high visibility during his campaign made him a more likely target. Alicia read about all of this on the pastor's wife's posts.

Un Mediated

On the Sunday morning of the threats, we signed up to join a semi-circle of nonviolent barrier cars in front of the pastor's house, while he and his wife broadcast online (this was during Covid). The other people we met in the barrier circle were, of course, from that pastor's church.

The following week, we tuned in online to that church's gatherings. I heard the pastor open with these words: "We are a community seeking to be expansive and inclusive, where everyone has a place at the table. We believe that no matter your tradition or background, how you identify, who you love, or where you are on life's journey, you are a beloved child of God." Those words, that vision – it was like a butterfly landed on my nose. It was a vivid contrast to my former faith life.

Soon enough we were listening to those words regularly, while gathered with the other non-violent barrier people on Sunday mornings. We saw that they were committed to peace and spiritual safety not just in the pastor's driveway, but in all of life and faith. We could feel that safety for ourselves. Eventually I entered the process of "exploration and discernment" for ordination in the United Church of Christ. Part of that exploration involved class-time.

One day, three pastors from the UCC joined our class in a panel discussion. One was an African American male, who was pastoring two white congregations. Another was a female who identified as Queer and had married another woman. The third was an older white male, who was on the conservative side of the UCC continuum and openly disagreed, on the Bible's terms, with same-sex marriage. The class time discussion was wide-ranging, but at one point the white conservative pastor said, "I want to make it clear that all three of us love each other in Christ. We are in a weekly Bible study together. We pray together. We deeply disagree in our views, *and* we are deep friends in Christ."

Never had I seen such a thing in all my life. My eyes were stinging with tears. This looked and sounded like Jesus to me. These people knew how to abide with each other in faith. My heart was captivated.

From that moment, I left the realm of "exploration," and entered the ordination process full-on. I completed the studies, submitted to the interviews, and was granted ordination in the United Church of Christ. These days, I express that ordination as a hospice chaplain. Sometimes I offer a sermon. Alicia now serves on the Leadership Team for our church.

Strange to say, but this doesn't mean I have all my faith questions answered. Even now, I am somewhat numb. I do not look to my pastor, my church, my denomination, or a worship service to solve my lostness. It's just this, I think: My soul can breathe. There is a place of community for me while I talk to God from my ditch, and while I dumpster dive. Within that community, there is wide latitude for doctrinal, religious, and life-choice differences. With the core teachings of Jesus in mind, we speak openly against

Un Mediated

racism and religious violence. The pastor does not impose; he thinks out loud. Nobody tries to dazzle anybody else. There is no light show. If there is food, it's because someone baked cookies. If we sing a song, it expresses divine love, human dignity, and justice. I can be there and serve there with no sense that human hands are groping my soul or interrupting the unmediated love of God. It contributes to my overall sense of spiritual freedom.

In my life, and in my work as a chaplain, and as an ordained pastor, sometimes, just sometimes, when I least expect it, I find myself in proximity to another person and suddenly the love of Christ compels me. In that moment, there is no religious rule or potentate to tell me "No." Instead, my church and denomination say, "Yes!" There is no limit to God's love in and through me. Without human restriction, I can administer God's grace in its various forms. For me, this is the glorious freedom of a child of God, pure and simple.

This is not a sales pitch for the UCC. It's just our journey and how it worked for us. I tell you this because I believe you have a place, somewhere, in the universal, diverse, and beautiful Body of Christ.

My only challenge and encouragement is: Don't settle for a small, mean, or violent vision of God. "Expansive and inclusive," our pastor says. That's what you're after.

I believe God will lead you to it.

UnMediated

Simple **Faith**. Pure **Love**.

Un Mediated

Simple **Faith**. Pure **Love**.

Conclusion

Summary

I believe The Church, in dementia, has given its heart in idolatry to Donald Trump. I protested this, and in the process, I lost my faith. In the whirlwind, I got stripped down. I stumbled into a way of thinking and being. I am learning as I go.

I meet God sometimes, but not in a humanly manufactured religious atmosphere. I find Jesus, rather, in weakness and death - in the synapse of human hearts, together.

I reject the false, wealth-based, violence-based, nation-and-empire-based Mosaic religion which is gaining strength and imposing its hellish power and its mental and spiritual illness upon our nation and world.

If you are losing your faith, if you are sitting in church feeling like a corpse, knowing in your bones that *it is where Jesus is not,* I would recommend: Get out. Light your own fuse and fly. Go anywhere else. Refuse to roll in that dirt anymore.

It's OK. You are not crazy. Your soul is working just fine. Go! It will be difficult, but God will not fail you.

Rise each day and lift your soul to God. Enter human suffering with an open, curious heart. Keep human compassion at the center. Dwell there. As Jesus, the Cosmic Good Samaritan, promised, you will meet him there.

If you have time, energy, or desire left after that, by all means, find a gathering for human companionship. Find a good, humble, kind-hearted, courageous pastor. Find a place that proclaims a salvation of justice on earth, as it is in heaven. Find a safe place where everyone is welcome at the table.

It's like this: You are a small plant, fed and nourished in light and love. You are in God's hand, suspended there. No preacher or institution rules your soul.

You are sustained and upheld by simple faith, and pure love. Unmediated.

Suffering to Stand against Religious Trumpism

I implore you to oppose Donald Trump and Religious Trumpism. What this means for you, I do not know. I suspect it will cost us; that we will experience some kind of suffering and loss. Jesus rejected the corrupt, earthly religion promoted at point of sword by hyper-religious, nationalistic zealots, and they killed him for it.

I am afraid, sometimes. I wonder, when it counts, if I will roll in the dirt again.

I hope, this time, to stand.

Un Mediated

Simple **Faith**. Pure **Love**.

UnMediated

Simple Faith. Pure Love.

Endnotes

1- For the text of the article promoting Old Testament violence, see Joseph Rigney, "Empathy, Feminism, and the Church" in *American Reformer.* January 26, 2024).

   https://americanreformer.org/2024/01/empathy-feminism-and-the-church/

2- For a snapshot of Ottawa Impact in my County, see Sam Landstra, "Deeply Religious, Divided: Ottawa Impact and the Christians in Their County" from Fox17, January 5, 2024.

   https://www.fox17online.com/news/local-news/lakeshore/ottawa/deeply-religious-divided-ottawa-impact-and-the-christians-in-their-county

3- For the film trailer for *God and Country*, see "God & Country – Official Trailer (2024)." YouTube, uploaded by IGN Movie Trailers, 8 December 2023.

   https://www.youtube.com/watch?v=-MFQ2uESrjU

4- For a review of the film *God and Country*, see "God and Country" by Christy Berghoef in *Reformed Journal*, March 20, 2024.

   https://reformedjournal.com/god-and-country/

5- See Russell Moore's *Losing Our Religion* (Sentinel 2023), 7.

6- See Amar D. Peterman's "Taylor Swift Needs Fog Machines. God Does Not" in *Sojourners*, July 14, 2023. *https://sojo.net/articles/taylor-swift-needs-fog-machines-god-does-not*

7- For descriptions of Trump's enjoyment of January 6, see Patricia Zengerle and Richard Cowan, "Trump Watched Jan. 6 U.S. Capitol Riot Unfold on TV, Ignored Pleas to Call for Peace" in *Reuters*, July 22, 2022. *https://www.reuters.com/world/us/us-capitol-probes-season-finale-focus-trump-supporters-three-hour-rage-2022-07-21/*

Also see Peter Wade, "'Look at All Those People Fighting for Me': Trump 'Gleefully' watched Jan. 6 Riot, Says Former Press Secretary" in *Rolling Stone*, January 6, 2022. *https://www.rollingstone.com/politics/politics-news/stephanie-grisham-trump-gleefully-watched-jan-6-1280113/*

8- For more on the billboard "A Son is Given," see Jack Beresford, "Billboard Comparing Donald Trump to Jesus Christ Removed" in *Newsweek*, September 15, 2021. *https://www.newsweek.com/billboard-comparing-donald-trump-jesus-christ-removed-georgia-1629381*

9- For a sampling of Christian imagery at the Capitol on January 6, 2021, see Tyler Merbler's photograph "MAGA Jesus" on *Uncivil Religion*, January 6, 2021. *https://uncivilreligion.org/home/media/maga-jesus*

9- Gina Ciliberto and Stephanie Russell-Kraft, "They Invaded the Capitol Saying 'Jesus Is My Savior. Trump Is My President'" in *Sojourners*, January 7, 2021. *https://sojo.net/articles/they-invaded-capitol-saying-jesus-my-savior-trump-my-president*

9- Jack Jenkins, "Police Officer Says Capitol Rioters 'Perceived Themselves to Be Christians'" in *The Roys Report*, July 27, 2021. *https://julieroys.com/capitol-rioters-perceived-themselves-christians/*

10- For comparisons of Trump's sufferings to those of Jesus, see Andrew Stanton, "Donald Trump Shares Jesus Comparison While in Court" in *Newsweek*, March 25, 2024. *https://www.newsweek.com/donald-trump-shares-jesus-comparison-while-court-stormy-daniels-1883109*

11- For Dan Deitrich's song to The Church, see "Hymn for the 81%." YouTube, uploaded by Daniel Deitrich, 28 September 2022. *https://www.youtube.com/watch?v=WidUnxxovD8*

12- See Philip Yancey, *What's So Amazing About Grace?* (Zondervan 1997), 142.

13- See David James Duncan, *Sun House* (Little, Brown 2023), 149.

UnMediated

Simple Faith. Pure Love.

Acknowledgements

Dr. Christy Berghoef read the first draft and said, "This needs to get out into the world!" She was the first to make me believe I could, and should, publish it. Christy did all the photography and gave advice along the way.

Doug Brouwer read the first draft and instantly became a warm and enthusiastic encourager, an advocate, and a friend.

Rod & Alli Colburn found Alicia and me when we were in a whirlwind and gave us loving shelter. Rod read the first draft and became a fireball of encouragement and editorial advice.

Stacey Graham, our dear friend, read the draft and, from way over in Italy, sent words of heartfelt, passionate, and tearful encouragement.

**Because of the people mentioned above,
I dared to publish this book.**

Thanks to . . .

Jacob Schepers, who applied his generous heart, powerful mind, and professional editorial touch to every aspect of this project.

Kris & Vern Swierenga, and **Jeff & Vicki Meyer,** for walking with us, and loving us, through the whirlwind.

Gord Baas, the only person who writes longer texts than me, for sending razor sharp insight, with unfailing humor, about Religious Trumpism and its effects.

UnMediated

Jeff Munroe (editor of *The Reformed Journal* and author of *Telling Stories in the Dark*) for lighting a spark within me, opening doors for me, and mentoring me. Thanks also to the *Reformed Journal* community for reading things I wrote about my journey and for encouraging me along the way.

Tim Gilman, my personal Tony the Tiger, who kept saying, "This'll be GREAT!," and who went on, with unfailing patience and love, to so beautifully put this book into form.

Doug Pagitt and **Brian D. McLaren** for giving me their time, encouragement, and support.

Scott & Judy VanderZwaag, who believed in the project, and gave their loving investment and encouragement.

About the Author

Keith Mannes has been a pastor for over thirty years. He is now ordained in the United Church of Christ, and expresses that ordination as a Hospice Chaplain.

He has authored numerous articles, including in *Leadership Journal* and The *Reformed Journal*. He and his wife Alicia have three children and four grandchildren.

www.ingramcontent.com/pod-product-compliance
Lightning Source LLC
Chambersburg PA
CBHW020654060526
44119CB00069B/33